I0879890

The Great Migration and the Democratic Party

KENESHIA N. GRANT

The Great Migration and the Democratic Party

Black Voters and the Realignment of American Politics in the 20th Century

TEMPLE UNIVERSITY PRESS
Philadelphia • Rome • Tokyo

TEMPLE UNIVERSITY PRESS
Philadelphia, Pennsylvania 19122
tupress.temple.edu

Published 2020

Library of Congress Cataloging-in-Publication Data

Names: Grant, Keneshia Nicole, 1983– author.
Title: The great migration and the Democratic party : Black voters and the realignment of American politics in the 20th century / Keneshia Grant, Syracuse University.
Description: Philadelphia : Temple University Press, 2020. | Includes bibliographical references and index. | Summary: "This book examines how the mass movement of African Americans from the South to the North from approximately 1915 to 1970—the movement commonly known as the Great Migration—helped change the relative positions and policy stances on racial politics for the major American political parties."— Provided by publisher.
Identifiers: LCCN 2019020033 (print) | LCCN 2019980416 (ebook) | ISBN 9781439917459 (cloth : alk. paper) | ISBN 9781439917466 (paperback : alk. paper) | ISBN 9781439917473 (ebook)
Subjects: LCSH: African Americans—Migrations—History—20th century. | African Americans—Politics and government—20th century. | Party affiliation—United States. | Democratic Party (U.S.) | United States—Politics and government—20th century.
Classification: LCC E185.6 .G74 2020 (print) | LCC E185.6 (ebook) | DDC 323.1196/073—dc23
LC record available at https://lccn.loc.gov/2019020033
LC ebook record available at https://lccn.loc.gov/2019980416

♾ The paper used in this publication meets the requirements of the American National Standard for Information Sciences—Permanence of Paper for Printed Library Materials, ANSI Z39.48-1992

Printed in the United States of America

9 8 7 6 5 4 3 2

For Gary Paul and Kristi Andersen

Contents

Acknowledgments

Five years old, capable, and excited about learning, I showed up for first grade at Royal Palm Elementary School wholly unprepared. Much of my early education was an uphill battle, aided in large part by teachers who cared deeply about their work and my success. As I got older, and better at reading and writing, school became more enjoyable. Even so, never could I have imagined my current life as a professor and published author.

As an undergraduate at Florida A&M University, I learned that hard work could get dressed as an excellent student. At Syracuse University, the same lesson—that grit could outperform a lack of preparation—carried me through to my doctorate. At both institutions, I met people whose investment in me made this book and my career possible. Without Gary Paul, I would have had no notion of a doctoral degree or of myself as a professor. His question "Who will teach in the HBCUs if you all don't?" made me think about my commitment to historically Black colleges and universities and about myself as an educator in a whole new light. Gary cheered me on through graduate school and through my time as an assistant professor, and for that, I am thankful. Without Kristi Andersen, my time as a student at Syracuse and my academic journey thereafter would have been much less direct. Kristi's lessons, which came through her example as often as they came directly, have stuck with me over the years. Many times while writing this and other works, I have heard her voice as I tried to strike a balance in my writing: "You don't have to try to 'sound smart' if you have a strong idea" and "Words matter." She has been there to read (and edit!) countless drafts of my work, to encourage me when I needed it, and to push me when that was necessary too. Gary and Kristi are my friends and colleagues now, but they will always be etched in my mind as the people who deserve my deepest gratitude for my career. For that reason, I dedicate this book to them.

Many people helped me produce this work. I thank Aaron Javsicas, editor in chief at Temple University Press, for visiting Howard University to find our stories. I am grateful, too, for his professionalism and transparency, which set the bar high for me as a first-time book author. I also thank the rest of the team at Temple University Press, especially Joan S. Vidal, and Heather Wilcox at Second Glance Editorial for their contribution in polishing this book. I was lucky to have reviewers who gave me valuable feedback, which strengthened this work. I thank them for their questions, which challenged me to think about the balance of power in broad terms and to use available electoral data to tell Chicago's story. I thank Jeffrey Gonda, Seth Jolly, Tom Keck, Quinn Mulroy, and the rest of the 2008–2014 faculty of the Syracuse University Department of Political Science. They supported me through the dissertation process and have continued to support my ideas and ambitions long after my time at the Maxwell School.

My thanks go to the staff of the Chicago Board of Elections, including Joan Agnew, Delilah Smith, "Chop," and the rest of the Pershing Street warehouse team, who all made a tedious task very enjoyable. The interior and cover illustrations extend from the work and generosity of librarians and professionals at Getty, the Associated Press, the Library of Congress, the Jacob and Gwendolyn Knight Lawrence Foundation, and the Phillips Collection. I extend a special thank-you to Candy Martinez, a Howard University alumna, who created the map of the migration streams.

The Howard University community has been an important partner in the production of this book as well. Michael Fauntroy pushed me to think about my research agenda as a series of books rather than a series of articles. Rick Seltzer provided helpful feedback and suggestions about the work in its early stages and in the analysis of the Chicago chapter. Such opportunities as Howard University's Summer Writing Academy, Summer Research Fellowship, and Alternative Spring Break provided space for me to think and write. Very importantly, the Summer Writing Academy and Summer Research Fellowship furnished monetary support for this project. Dr. Wayne A. I. Frederick and the office of the Howard University president contributed a great deal to my comfortable transition into academia and my success as an assistant professor. Research assistance from my 2017–2018 undergraduate American state and local government classes was invaluable as I worked to compile data on the political activity of the migrants who became elected officials.

Of course, life—mine in particular—is not all work. Friends and family, who have varying levels of familiarity with my work, have been consistent in their extraordinary levels of support. I thank my biggest cheerleaders, my mom and dad, Joan Grant and Ringo Cayard. My mom was my advocate in those early "capable but unprepared" years. She knew that I could rise to the challenge of academic success. I will never forget the time we spent passing the spelling book back and forth on the way home from school after her very long workdays. I thought my curiosity about politics had been awakened by my mother, who made me watch WSVN news every morning, but I later learned that it was probably genetic. My dad, who is involved in politics himself and comes from a political family, constantly challenges me to think about the world from a perspective outside my own. I am a better political scientist, citizen, and person because of his influence.

I am grateful to my network of friends, who have been cheering me on since the beginning; in particular, Kenyetta Harrison and WhoGotDaBody have provided solace when it comes time to unwind from work and enjoy life. The day before my classes began at Syracuse University, Phyllis Green asked me whether the Great Migration was related to politics in any way. Although I swiftly responded that it was "history and sociology stuff," her question, which stuck with me as I wrestled with the American government literature, is part of the reason this book exists. Ashley Milton, Marie Johns, and the Metropolitan AME Church (MAMEC) family were important writing and motivation partners as I worked to get my ideas off the ground. To Ashley, I offer gratitude for sitting with me for all those hours. To MAMEC, I extend thanks for the love, space, and free Wi-Fi.

I thank my scholar sisters—Niambi Carter, Jarpa Dawuni, Pearl Ford Dowe, Sheena Harris, Keesha Middlemass, and Rachel Sigman. Each of these women has always been happy to share her resources when I was without. They have also offered an ear when I needed to vent and a shoulder when I needed someone to lean on. I thank everyone who supported me from afar via social media. Special thanks go to Andrea Price, who found the birthplace of Illinois state representative George T. Kersey, which had eluded me for many months.

Last, but not least, I thank my partner, Brandon Hogan. A philosopher and lawyer by training, Hogan helped tremendously with revisions to the Introduction and Chapter 1, through intellectual sparring matches that made me clarify my arguments and positions. With little tolerance for my own doubts, Hogan has also been there to support me in the moments when I questioned whether and how I might complete this and other projects. All in all, he has been careful to ensure that our lives include a thoughtful mix of work, fun, and love.

—Keneshia N. Grant, Ph.D.

The Great Migration and the Democratic Party

Introduction

By 1907, Edward Austin Johnson was fed up with the system of racism in North Carolina that limited his ability to participate in politics (E. Johnson 1942). Just a decade earlier, he and other Black Republicans were working in coalition with white Progressives in the Populist Party. He served on the Republican Party's executive committee in the Fourth District and had been a delegate to three Republican National Conventions.[1] *In 1896, Johnson was elected as an alderman in Raleigh. However, in the White Supremacy Campaign of 1898, the white members of the Populist Party broke ranks with Black Republicans to join political forces with southern Democrats. Johnson lost his seat in the city council, but he remained involved in local politics through his ties to the Republican Party. From 1899 to 1907, he worked as an assistant to the federal attorney for the district of eastern North Carolina. Although he was still active in politics, he despaired of the political situation in his home state. So in 1907, Johnson decided to migrate to New York City and establish a legal practice.*[2] *He became involved in local politics immediately, arguing that New York City's political parties should nominate Black people to represent the rapidly growing Black areas of the city. Eventually, he was appointed Republican Party chair for the predominately Black Nineteenth Assembly district in Harlem. In 1917, Johnson became the first Black person elected to the New York state legislature.*

While Johnson was preparing to take his seat in the New York legislature, Clarence Metcalfe and Marie Attaway were getting ready to leave their home in Atlanta with their seven-year-old son, Ralph. Clarence and Marie—a stockyard worker and a seamstress—believed they could do better for themselves and their son in Chicago. That same year, a clothier named Richard Brown was also contemplating ways to make a better life for his family. Richard moved his wife and daughter, Alice and Cora, a relatively short distance from their home in Bessemer, Alabama, to Birmingham. But the urban South proved less lucrative than Richard had hoped, so on the advice of his in-laws, he moved the family north to Detroit, Michigan.

Unlike Johnson, Ralph Metcalfe and Cora Brown did not actively choose to participate in the Great Migration. Their parents made the decision for them, just as many other Black parents did when they moved their children to try to provide access to a better life. Ralph and Cora thrived in the North. Ralph graduated from high school in Chicago and attended Marquette University as a student athlete. Eventually, he became an Olympic sprinter. After a career as an athlete, war veteran, and university instructor in Louisiana, Ralph returned to Chicago to work as the director of the civil rights department of the Chicago Commission on Human Relations. Cora also did well in high school. Like many migrants of her generation, she returned to the South to attend a historically Black college, studying sociology at Fisk University in Nashville. Cora returned to Detroit immediately after graduation and began a career as a social worker. Cora's success, like Ralph's, also extended into her adult life and translated into a strong record of public service.

In 1952, Ralph and Cora experienced another similar life event—both won campaigns for elected political office. Ralph became an alderman representing the Third Ward of Chicago on the city council. This political victory would be the first of many during his long career. Cora became the first Black woman to serve in any state senate after winning her seat in Michigan. The decision to migrate to the North powerfully shaped Ralph's and Cora's lives throughout their careers and political trajectories. This book is about the ways that such people as Edward Johnson, Ralph Metcalfe, and Cora Brown changed politics in the North through their Great Migration.

Where we live matters. However, when we think about the implications of place and home, we often focus on the relatively trivial. Hometowns influence how we speak and what we eat: consider a southern drawl or New England clam chowder. Americans with good "midwestern values" or a "New York state of mind" might say where we are from influences how we interact with people. For Black Americans, the implications of one's location have always been far more serious than an accent or food preferences. Location has meant the difference between slavery and freedom, discrimination and equality, or poverty and economic opportunity.

Where Black people live has also been an important determinant of their ability to participate in political processes. Under normal circumstances, American citizens' formal participation in politics can begin when they reach voting age. However, Black Americans living in the South have always faced tremendous impediments to political participation. When Reconstruction ended in 1877, Black suffrage came under siege. Southern legislatures implemented laws to weaken or eliminate the Black vote, including grandfather clauses and white primaries.[3] Outside the political apparatus, southerners used violence and intimidation to diminish the Black vote. Because most of the Black population lived in the South and faced these barriers to voting, only a small percentage of Black Americans in the South participated in electoral politics before the Voting Rights Act of 1965.

From 1915 to 1965, more than six and a half million Black Americans left their homes in the rural South to resettle in the North through a movement called the Great Migration. Together with the frustrations brought by denial of fundamental rights and privileges, restricted opportunities for economic mobility drove Black people out of the South in large numbers. Their migration fundamentally altered the American demographic landscape by shifting almost half of the Black population from primarily southern and rural places to the urban North. Migrants went to big, far-away cities, such as Chicago, New York, and Philadelphia. In some instances, they moved out of the larger cities to settle in places that were just a bit smaller, such as Indianapolis, Cleveland, and Pittsburgh. They also moved to places that bordered the South, such as St. Louis, Topeka, and Washington, D.C.

The difference in laws between the North and the South created a political coming of age for Black migrants. Seeing political participation as a badge of honor and hallmark of success in northern life, migrants registered to vote in large numbers. Northern parties and candidates worked to gain Black support through their election campaigns, and the parties expected Black voters to turn out to vote for their nominees on Election Day. Further, unlike in the South, Black transplants to the North had the opportunity to directly participate in politics by holding elected and appointed positions.

The central question of *The Great Migration and the Democratic Party* is "How did the Great Migration influence American politics in northern cities?" I argue that the Great Migration changed how Democratic Party elites interacted with Black communities in northern cities. My argument consists of four premises: (1) Black Americans moved out of the South into the North through the Great Migration. In many instances, they settled in large urban areas. (2) The migration changed Black citizens' ability to participate in politics because many barriers to participation in the South did not exist in the North. The Great Migration effectively created a new pool of eligible voters. (3) Many white Democratic politicians came to believe that Black voters could help them reach their electoral goals. They often believed that Black voters might swing the balance of power in elections and that a unified Black voting bloc might help them win factional disputes during primary elections. Where they were not able to tip the balance of power, Black voters might be important coalition partners in elections. (4) White Democratic politicians changed their campaign strategies and positions to manage Black support because of their belief that Black voters were important. In some instances, that management was positive, with some white politicians trying to encourage Black political participation. In other instances, that management was negative, with some white politicians actively working to suppress Black political activity. Therefore, the Great Migration led to changes in northern political parties, especially the Democratic Party. This book contributes to our understanding of the fifty-year period from 1915 to 1965 by expanding how we think about the Great Migration, twentieth-century American state and local politics, and party development. *The Great Migration and the Democratic Party* adds to the existing literature by framing the Great Migration as an important economic and social event that had serious political consequences. Further, it adds to the American politics literature by emphasizing the Great Migration as one phenomenon, among many, that contributed to changes in political parties during the twentieth century.

Plan of the Book

The chapters that follow describe the impact of the Great Migration on politics in three American cities from 1915 to 1965.[4] Chapter 1 describes my argument and methods in detail. Then, the chapter engages the American politics literature on realignment to discuss how and why parties change their positions on issues in two ways. First, I assert that demographic changes are important to explain party position change. Some of the literature on secular realignment considers demography by questioning how movers are influenced by politics in a place. Instead of questioning how a place changes people, I take the position that a large influx of potential new voters could lead to change in a political environment. In other words, I question how people change the politics of a place. Further, I consider demographic trends among Black people as an important explanation for change in politics outside the South. Second, concerning the "why" of party change,

I argue that change most likely occurs when parties believe that altering issue positions will have a positive impact on electoral outcomes. In other words, parties adjust when they believe that the benefits of changing outweigh the costs of remaining the same. Parties construct expectations of costs and benefits on the basis of feedback from members of the party coalition, who may express opinions directly or through their votes. Chapter 1 frames established Black residents of the North and migrants as an increasingly important part of the Democratic coalition, who forced the party to change by voting and pushing their agenda through groups of like-minded individuals.

Chapter 2 draws on scholarship from historians and sociologists to provide detail about the causes and consequences of the Great Migration. The first half of the chapter covers the Black migrations in America that preceded the Great Migration. The second half of the chapter focuses on the Great Migration, including (1) the timing of the migration, which scholars generally describe as happening in two waves, (2) the factors that encouraged migration, and (3) how the distribution of the Black American population changed because of the migration. This chapter also provides the reader with background information about the migrants that is necessary to understand the rest of the story. Who were they? What motivated them to leave the South? What were their experiences once they moved to the North?

Chapters 3, 4, and 5 describe the political situations in Detroit, New York, and Chicago—three cities with vastly different political environments. In these chapters, I first rely on local newspaper accounts, political analyses, and scholarly work about the cities to explain how changes in the electorate shaped mayoral candidates' positions on issues of importance to the Black community. I describe how candidates and parties changed their positions—and in some instances adopted new ones—to manage electoral support as the Black population grew in these cities. Second, I describe the direct political involvement of Black elected officials, including the migrants themselves. I use official government records, news media, books, and dissertations to pull together a data set of all[5] Black elected officials in Chicago, New York, and Detroit from

1915 to 1965. I then identify which of the Black elected officials were migrants. Finally, I consider the legislative priorities of Black elected officials and highlight instances when the migrants had distinct legislative priorities.

This book's Conclusion provides a summary and a bit of epilogue. The period following the Great Migration saw a wave of Black electoral power across the United States, including election to the highest local offices in the cities under consideration here. The Conclusion also introduces new ways to think about the contemporary impact of Black migration on American politics. The children and grandchildren of Great Migration participants have been returning to the South since the 1970s in a movement called Return Migration. This new generation of migrants is demonstrating preferences for metropolitan areas in the South, such as Charlotte, Atlanta, and Houston. Their movement raises important questions about their potential to influence politics at the subnational level. Further, it raises questions about these migrants' potential to change presidential candidates' approach to campaigning for Black support in the South. Thus, the Conclusion sketches some of our first understandings of the political impact of the Black population's move back south.

1

Party Change and the Great Migration

Models of Party Change

Moving from one place to another is common for most Americans.[1] Although the decision to move is often wrapped up in economic or family considerations, choosing to move has political implications for the movers and for the political systems where they settle. This situation has been especially true for Black Americans, whose ability to participate in politics often has been limited by where they live. In the pre–Civil War South, white people barred Black Americans from political activity as a condition of their enslavement. When slavery ended, Black participation in electoral politics was possible for a time, as formerly enslaved people voted and held political office during Reconstruction. However, Black Americans' ability to freely participate in politics came to a grinding halt following the Grand Bargain of 1877. Republicans agreed to Democrats' demands for removal of federal troops from the South in exchange for concession of the presidency to the Republican candidate, Rutherford B. Hayes. The end of Reconstruction led to the widespread and pervasive disenfranchisement of Black citizens for decades to come. Despite Black Americans' constitutional right to vote through the Fifteenth Amendment, white primaries, grandfather clauses, violence, and a host of other tactics stood between Black voters and ballot boxes almost immediately following the end of federal occupation of the South.

The Great Migration unlocked Black Americans' ability to participate as full citizens in our democracy, in many instances making them political participants for the first time: "The move was more than simple migration and change in folkways for blacks, it was a move, almost literally, from no voting to voting" (Brooks 1974: 17). When migrants arrived in the North, they were often anxious to participate in politics and therefore contributed to an expansion of the electorate in northern areas. Thus, any explanation of urban politics in the North or evolution of political positions on race is incomplete without an explicit acknowledgment of the Great Migration.

The overarching goal of this book is to highlight the Great Migration as a factor that shaped party development in America and to expand our thinking about the Great Migration by focusing on migrants as political actors. As northern electorates changed, political actors—parties and politicians—responded to the changes in the electorate in a number of ways: (1) they took positions to attract support from Black voters; (2) they worked to mobilize Black voters during election campaigns; and (3) in some instances, when they were unwilling to meet Black demands, they worked to limit the power of Black voters by demobilizing the population.

In the first part of this chapter, I describe my argument in detail. I also discuss the methods I use to answer the question of the political impact of the Great Migration. In the second part of this chapter, I situate the Great Migration in our current conceptions of political change. I begin by considering what scholars in fields outside political science have to say about the role of politics in the Great Migration. Next, I engage the party change literature about the ways large-scale changes in the population impact politics in states and communities. Then, I consider what the party change literature has to say about the Great Migration.

Argument

The central argument of this work is that northward migration created Black Americans' ability to participate in politics, thus changing the political landscape in at least two important ways: (1) northern politicians' interactions with Black voters changed as the population grew and (2) the Great Migration led to an increase in the number of Black elected officials. At the very beginning of the twentieth century, parties and politicians paid only slight and inconsistent attention to Black voters. Election to political office was not commonplace for Black Americans. But by the end of the migration, candidates and parties believed that they must address Black voters in their electoral calculations if they were going to be competitive.

Writing in 1960, James Q. Wilson argued that entry into politics in Great Migration cities varied and depended on three factors: "(a) the rate of in-migration, (b) the density of the Negro area, and (c) the size of the basic political unit" (25). I agree with his notion and add that the degree to which parties and politicians were responsive to migrants differed on the basis of (1) the interaction of the spatial distribution of Black people with the rules for election to office and (2) the degree of party cohesion. In cities, Black populations were most effective when political systems were organized by small, residence-based electoral units and when those units were segregated by race. At the subnational and national levels, migrants were most influential in elections when the non-Black electorate was split and the Black electorate was unified.[2]

A party's response to migrants was positive if the party did not have any choice except to respond positively; the Black population was too big to ignore; the Black population lived in small, homogenous units; the party's goals were aligned with the goals of the Black population; or the Black voters were the balance of power.[3] Black voters might be the balance of power if the party was split into competing factions or if the electorate was evenly split on issues. When the response was positive, a party would register and mobilize Black voters, allow participation in the party organization, or nominate Black candidates for office.

In some instances, party responses to the influx of Black voters were negative. Parties responded negatively when the Black vote would prevent the dominant party from winning; Black voters' goals were not aligned with a party's goals/aims; or the population of voters in the Northern cities where migrants settled was composed of large, heterogeneous subunits and the Black voting bloc was not large enough to be consequential. A party's negative response might involve excluding Black citizens from party decision making, constructing barriers to voting, nominating whites for offices in Black areas, demobilizing voters, or taking racist positions to attract/mobilize white voters. Although the Black community did not always get its fair share of benefits from the substantial role it played in getting candidates elected to office, candidates were forced to consider responding to the presence of Black residents, take public positions on racial issues, mobilize (or, in some instances, suppress) the Black vote as it expanded, and work with Black community leaders and politicians.

The second important consequence of the Great Migration is the immediate increase in the number of Black elected officials, many of whom were migrants. The number of Black people in elected positions throughout the United States was miniscule at the beginning of the Great Migration period. As the number of Black residents grew in northern cities, so did the likelihood that Black candidates would win elections because political parties nominated them for office or because they made individual decisions to run. As political office holders, Black elected officials could amplify the voices of Black Americans in ways that were not possible before the Great Migration unlocked their political potential. In other words, the Great Migration also created a class of legislators who had the ability to bring the concerns of the Black community onto agendas in state legislatures and in city councils.

One of the goals of this book is to highlight the agency of

Black people in the story of twentieth-century party development. Black people exist only in the background in many of the works about change in American political parties. When we do highlight Black people, we most often think about them in the aggregate through their roles in interest groups, civil rights organizations, or religious bodies. Another way of highlighting Black political participants is to focus on the leaders who represented civic and religious organizations or media outlets. *The Great Migration and the Democratic Party* builds on previous work by highlighting the role of individual Black political office holders in driving attention to the problems faced by Black Americans during this period.

Scholarly Treatments of the Great Migration

Scholars in fields outside political science—especially historians and sociologists—have written extensively about the Great Migration. The earliest work in this area details migrants' move northward and what they encountered when they reached the North. Later scholarship considers the role of the Great Migration in shaping northern communities and patterns of housing. More recent work examines the impact of the Great Migration on class formation in northern cities.[4] The most popular works on the Great Migration are large in scope and describe various parts of the migration across cities and over long periods of time. The most famous of these are narratives. Nicholas Lemann (1992) and Isabel Wilkerson (2010) each describe the Great Migration in detail through the lives of three migrants. James Gregory (2006) departs from these traditions by using social-science methods to consider a range of topics in *The Southern Diaspora*—including migrants' culture and participation in northern communities through work, religious organizations, and politics. Most often, research on migrants' politics is located in works about individual cities or writing about labor and civil rights issues of cities. One of my aims in this book is to create a separate space for consideration of politics during the Great Migration.

Political Change in American Politics Literature

Like many before me, I assume that electoral victory is the primary goal of political parties (Downs 1957; Schattschneider 1942). "Thus all of a party's actions are aimed at maximizing votes and it treats policies merely as a means toward this end" (Downs 1957: 35). In other words, "parties formulate policies in order to win elections rather than win elections in order to formulate policies" (28). Specifically, parties take positions that will allow them to attract an electorally effective coalition (Karol 2009). As they work to construct winning coalitions, parties focus on particular groups of voters whose support they believe will be most helpful toward the goal of meeting the institutional requirements necessary for attaining a position and whose political needs will not cost them an outsized amount of support from the other groups in the existing coalition.

Rules Constrain Parties

Parties may decide to change their positions on the basis of losses, but they do not change arbitrarily. For example, the rules of the Electoral College (EC) constrain presidential candidates' and parties' behaviors as they choose which states to target and which voters they should seek. Presidential candidates rarely debate the facts of the EC system on the road to the presidency because the requirements for winning this office are clear and well understood by candidates and their supporters: a presidential candidate must earn a majority of EC votes to be elected president. To obtain these votes, a presidential candidate must win the popular vote of the state.[5] If no candidate is successful in reaching a majority, the House of Representatives decides the election. Although presidential candidates may like to win as many votes as possible, EC strategy is the basis of their approach to winning votes. Parties make changes to their coalitions that further the goal of achieving a majority of votes in the EC.[6] Scott James (2006: 15) describes this approach in *Presidents, Parties and the State*: "Political competition for the presidency induces political parties to give disproportionate political attention to those states that hold the balance of power in the Electoral College."

The same logic behind the strategic pursuit of votes applies at the state and local levels. Politicians are constrained by the rules of their election. As vote seekers, they take positions and interact with voters in ways that increase the likelihood that they will win their elections. Candidates who are running in smaller, homogeneous electoral districts—ward or council districts, for example—take positions tailored to suit the concerns and desires of those seats. On the other hand, candidates who have to account for larger segments of the population—those running in at-large elections or running for positions like mayor, for example—may moderate their positions to achieve election.

Over the course of the twentieth century, parties and candidates had to adjust their approach to vote seeking to account for changes in the electorate stemming from the Great Migration. Although Black men were granted the right to vote with the Fifteenth Amendment and Black women won the right to vote with the Nineteenth Amendment, the vast majority of them were not able to exercise those rights because they lived in the South. When they moved north, more of them were able to participate in politics. If party officials believed that Black voters may be the balance of power (BOP) in a state or local election and/or believed that it might be possible to use Black support as part of a coalition to win elections, then it should follow that local parties and candidates may have become more liberal on civil rights issues as a way to gain the electoral support of this voting bloc.

Parties are especially interested in recruiting groups whose ideological positions most closely align with their current programs. Northern political parties of the twentieth century were aware that Black voters presented a unique coalition opportunity because of their numbers. Moreover, on the basis of Black voters' reaction to the New Deal, Democrats understood that Black voters might be a group that was amenable to the new positions of the party—positions that increasingly advocated for expansion of the federal government's role in social welfare and civil rights issues.[7]

Party Position Change

Political scientists generally think about political change as occurring either in the electorate or in a party's organization. Change in the electorate refers to alterations in the way individuals or groups of individuals engage or interact with parties. Work in this area describes why people change their party affiliations or what factors motivate their decisions to participate in political processes. On the other hand, work about changes in elite level politics refers to the ways that parties and/or candidates construct or reshape their strategies or policy positions as they interact with the electorate and seek to build coalitions. These elite-level changes are the focus of this work.

The dominant debate about change in American political parties has been between scholars using the concepts of realignment and issue evolution. Realignment literature answers questions about the rate, level, and source of political change using two broad notions. In one—critical realignment—change occurs swiftly as the electorate demonstrates a preference for new political leadership (Key 1955). The changes that occur following a critical realignment are lasting and lead to new groupings in the electorate. In the other view—secular realignment—change occurs gradually. Political elites make gradual changes in response to shifts in opinions on issues and preferences of the electorate (Key 1959). Much of the other work in the field builds on these two conceptions of party change.

Coalition management is another way to think about realignment. John Petrocik (1981) defines three types of behavior as realignment: conversion, mobilization, and demobilization (31). His theory includes two dimensions of mobilization: one where independent voters develop a new party preference (31) and another where levels of turnout increase (32). Kristi Andersen (1979) applies the concept of mobilization to the Democratic Party's change in the 1930s. She demonstrates that what looked like conversion of large numbers of people to the Democratic Party was actually mobilization of immigrants who had not participated in politics previously or did not have strong attachments to either political party. The Democrats registered these "non-immunized" individuals to vote, moved them to the polls, and benefited from this expansion of the electorate.[8]

Although conversion has been the most popular way to describe the realignment of Black voters, Andersen's theory of mobilization instead of conversion as an explanation for increasing support for the Democratic Party fits this case well. At first glance, conversion makes sense as an explanation for change in the party affiliation of Black voters because most of them participated in politics as Republicans for the first part of the twentieth century. Many of those Republicans did "convert" to the Democratic Party during the New Deal era. However, the Great Migration transported millions of Black citizens—who were not able to participate in politics previously—to northern cities and effectively expanded the electorate to include Black people for the first time since Reconstruction. Therefore, what looks like a wholesale defection from the Republican Party by the Black electorate can also be understood as the Democratic Party's mobilization of newly arrived Black migrants.[9]

In line with ideas about mobilization and conversion, David Karol and others suggest coalition management as a motivation for parties' position changes on issues related to race and civil rights (Bawn et al. 2012; Karol 2009). According to these accounts, groups pressured parties to change their positions on race. On the one hand, labor, white liberal coalitions, and Black voters increased pressure on the Democratic Party at the subnational level to liberalize its positions on race (Feinstein and Schickler 2008). The Republican Party, on the other hand, became more conservative on racial issues in an effort to keep its business lobby happy (Karol 2009). The idea of coalition management is an excellent development in our thinking about party motivations for position changes. However, this coalition management scholarship does not include a detailed account of how the Great Migration contributed to a change in the electorate.

Punctuated equilibrium—an alternative to realignment—suggests that change occurs rapidly after a "fairly steady stationary state" and continues to occur gradually thereafter (Carmines and Stimson 1989: 13). Issue evolution, through punctuated equilibrium, has been the most popular description of the Democratic Party's development on racial issues. Elite actors are most important in Edward Carmines and James Stimson's account, which suggests that Democrats' change on racial issues was largely a function of congressional membership replacement (1989: 63). A large cohort of liberals, newly elected to congress in 1958 and 1964, supported federal intervention on civil rights issues and pushed for liberal legislation. The result was rapid progress on civil rights issues in the 1960s, in part because of generational replacement and changes in the opinions of elite actors.

But recent scholarship challenges several parts of this story, including the rate, timing, and level of change as well as the Democratic Party's motivations for shifting positions. For example, scholars have questioned Carmines and Stimson's use of 1963 as a critical moment. Revisionists argue that the change was slow, beginning in the 1930s and 1940s and then continuing through the 1960s. They also question the idea that changes on civil rights issues originated at the congressional and presidential levels. Instead, they propose that shifts in the party's position began at the state level and show how state party platforms became liberal sooner than national party platforms (Feinstein and Schickler 2008; Schickler 2016).

To the debates between elite replacement (Carmines and Stimson 1989) and coalition management (Feinstein and Schickler 2008; Karol 2009; Pearson, Feinstein, and Schickler 2010), we should add the Andersen (1979) and Petrocik (1981) models, which conceptualize change as a response to transformations in the electorate. I argue that the development of party positions on racial issues in the North was an instance of realignment caused by the expansion of the electorate and the mobilization of a previously inactive[10] population. Although I acknowledge the many other factors in the environment that contributed to the parties' changing and to Black voters' growing affinity for Democrats, my focus here is the impact of the Great Migration.

Recent accounts in the literature of party change go a long way toward clarifying our understanding of an important moment in

American politics. However, they neglect a key but frequently overlooked factor in the story of party change—demography. None of these works adequately connects changes in the spatial distribution of the population of American citizens to developments in the major parties' positions on race. By all accounts, the increase in the Black population had some effect on the way politics happened in the North. However, the works include only a brief mention of the Great Migration—seemingly one of obligation rather than a full acknowledgment of this event's critical importance. The demographic transformations brought by the Great Migration add nuance to our understanding of parties' position changes on civil rights and racial issues and are an important component of our collective understanding of party development.

Partisan Transformation: Compositional and Contextual Effects of the Great Migration

When scholars of American politics do concern themselves with matters of demography in their consideration of party changes, they ask questions about migration's influence on partisan competition and write about migration in terms of its effects on individuals (contextual/micropolitical effects) or on communities (compositional/macropolitical effects). Although this book is centrally concerned with political change at elite levels and the compositional effects of migration, assumptions about the contextual effects that underlie the argument are also worth discussing here.

The work on micropolitical change questions how migration changes the political behavior and opinions of the mover. In other words, are migrants changed by their new homes, or do they change the places where they settle? Angus Campbell et al. (1960) argue that people have strong opinions that do not change when they move. It follows that if enough people move, in-migrants may change politics in the places where they settle. Thad Brown (1988) offers an alternative: migrants change their political positions after they move if they encounter electorates with positions that are very different from theirs. In this scenario, it is more likely that people change when they encounter new places than it is that they change the politics of those places. However, I argue that Black migrants' political opinions—especially those related to civil rights—were sufficiently stable to lead to changes in northern politics rather than being changed by the northern political environment.

Contextual Effects

Political immunization is the idea that people are shaped by their earliest political participation. The more a person participates in politics, the more likely it is that her or his political beliefs will remain stable across time and space (McPhee and Ferguson 1962). Campbell et al. (1960) build on this idea of political immunization to suggest that the average migrant's political life is usually unchanged by his or her migration. Although Campbell et al. write that adults' political opinions persist in spite of their move, they note the participants in the Great Migration as an exception to this idea: "Most of the blacks who moved north also developed political values more like blacks born in the urban North" (452). They describe Black Americans as previously non-immunized and therefore more likely to mimic the political positions of their northern counterparts once they began to participate in politics.

This argument is problematic for at least two reasons. First, it is difficult to know whether northern-born Black people had ideas and positions that differed from the participants in the Great Migration. One of the big methodological challenges of work in this field is the overall lack of information about Black voters before the Voting Rights Act of 1965. Rarely did voting registrars record the race of voters. Also rare was the likelihood that pollsters might reach out to Black citizens to record their opinions on issues of the day. Second, Black Americans of the Great Migration period should not be lumped with other non-immunized populations of the twentieth century. Unlike European immigrants, participants in the Great Migration moved within their home country. Also, unlike other instances of internal migration in the United States—namely, the migration to the western territories—participants in the Great Migration were moving between jurisdictions that had equal political standing and authority. In other words, they were not leaving territories to go to states or leaving states to go to territories; they were moving between equal subnational jurisdictions.

Campbell et al. are correct when they say that Black migrants were non-immunized, in the sense that they had not formally participated in politics. However, unlike other eligible voters in the United States, potential Black voters in the South faced state-sanctioned barriers to their participation. Therefore, it should follow that their exclusion from the ballot box changed the nature of their political immunization. If Black voters could have participated but chose not to, or if Black voters had entered the system without any knowledge of American politics, then it would be fair to describe them as having been non-immunized voters without political attachments in the same way that we may describe other groups.[11] However, in most instances, Black voters' lack of political participation was not their choice. They did not express political opinions in elections because they were effectively barred from doing so in the South. Therefore, we should consider how Black Americans *might have* participated when we think about their political immunization and potential impact on politics in the North.

In describing political immunization for Black voters in the South before 1965, we should modify what we traditionally classify as an interaction with the political system to account for their limited access. For example, we know that Black voters initially showed strong preferences for the Republican Party as a function of the party's racially liberal positions and willingness to support Black political participation during Reconstruction. Many disliked the Democratic Party, which they associated with racist behavior. Therefore, we should expect migrants' party affiliation in the North to be based on that party's commitment to Black issues—or the fact that the party took positions that would have pleased these migrants—not on the positions of the Black people who lived in the area before migrants arrived in large numbers. Put another way, because political issues connected to race, civil rights, and antidiscrimination efforts were the most important for Black migrants, their commitment to the party with favorable racial positions should have persisted when they arrived in the North—even if the party label was different in the North than it was in the South.

Compositional Effects

Scholars writing the compositional effects literature consider how migration may change the makeup of electorates, including a distinct focus on the growth of the Republican Party in the South as a function of a growing number of northerners' migrating to the South (Black and Black 2002; Converse 1966; Frendreis 1989). Less has been written about changes in either party as a function of northward migration, and scholars rarely discuss the Great Migration in terms of its impact on the composition of northern electorates. However, many of the hallmarks of the work about political change in the South are present in the story of the Great Migration. As in the South from 1970 onward, parties in the North changed as the migration occurred between 1915 and 1965. In thinking about the changes to the electorate that occurred in this time, it is useful to think of Black migrants as having expanded the electorate in northern cities.

Thinking about the Great Migration and Cities

The Great Migration and the Democratic Party expands the literature that compares the political impact of the Great Migration in multiple cities. Scholars have frequently written about Chicago (Drake and Cayton 1962; Gosnell 1967; Grimshaw 1992; Wilson 1960), Detroit (Sugrue 1995; Thompson 2001), New York (Biondi 2003; Lewinson 1974), Philadelphia (Countryman 2007; Wolfinger 2007), and Los Angeles (Flamming 2005; Sides 2004). Extensive discussions of politics in these cities often exist in writings about the cities' labor and civil rights problems. These works most often focus on the story and political environment in one place, without engaging in comparison across the cities. Although Hanes Walton's chapter on Black politics and political machines in *Black Politics: A Theoretical and Structural Analysis* (1972) describes Black participation in politics in seven cities, including New York and Chicago, it does not describe similarities or differences between the cities in great detail. Chapter 12 of *Black Politics* includes some comparison of cities, but it is limited to ranking them in terms of high and low levels of Black representation on city councils in 1965 (217).[12] In *Black Men, White Cities* (1973), Ira Katznelson considers the impact of migration on New York and Chicago from 1900 to 1930. He describes a system that allowed Black people to participate politically but did not allow them access to the formal positions or rewards they merited on the basis of their levels of participation. In this book, I build on these two important works that describe the political situation in multiple cities by focusing on the Great Migration as a cause of change in subnational political systems.

Black people left the South for many destinations over the course of the Great Migration. In addition to the three cities covered in this book, other locations are noteworthy. For example, Black populations in California grew following Japanese internment and throughout the second wave of the Great Migration. Black people also settled in smaller cities throughout the North and the Midwest, on the basis of the potential for employment. The story of the Great Migration is not limited to the largest cities in the United States, although those receive most of our scholarly attention. In some instances, Black folks ended their migration outside major cities, in such places as Gary, Indiana, or East Orange, New Jersey. Migration to places in the Border South, such as Washington, D.C., and St. Louis, Missouri, also took place.

Of all the Great Migration cities, I choose to study Detroit, New York, and Chicago for a few reasons. First, I want to observe changes in politics over the course of the entire migration. Although I consider in other writing the political impact of the Great Migration on Los Angeles, I eliminate it and other western cities from discussion in this book because the Black population was not significant there until the mid-1950s.[13] Second, I choose cities with three different political environments, which allows me to examine how politicians, parties, and migrants responded differently in places with varying political structures. Third, each of these cities has available data about Black political participation. Although the secondary research on the cities does not usually address the Great Migration directly, enough writing about the Black populations—in general or the political histories of the cities—exists to let me put together a coherent account of the period.

Who Is a Migrant?

I define a migrant as any person living in the North and born in the South, where the South is defined as Alabama, Arkansas, Florida, Georgia, Kentucky, Louisiana, Mississippi, North Carolina, Oklahoma, South Carolina, Tennessee, Texas, and Virginia. Although some Black people came to the North during slavery or just after emancipation, the number of Black people in a northern city was nearly a direct reflection of the number of migrants in a city at the beginning of the period.[14] For example, in 1910, 77 percent of the Black people living in Chicago were migrants.[15] However, it is less reliable to think of all Black people in a northern state or city later in the twentieth century as migrants; migrants who arrived in the earlier part of the century would go on to have children who were native northerners and therefore not considered migrants for my purposes.

To estimate the number of migrants as separate from the total population of Black northerners, I turn to U.S. census data: "The reports on state of birth of the native population, which have been published at each census since 1850, and have shed some light on the movement of the population" (United States Census 1940). I do not attempt to separate migrants according to the length of time they were in the North because I assume that being a migrant is a permanent status. In other words, a person who was born in the South but moved to the North through migration will always be shaped by that experience. Black migrants to the North "lived, worked, socialized, and worshipped primarily among other blacks from the South" (Gottlieb 1996: 210). Therefore, there is reason to believe that they had their identities as migrants reinforced after they arrived in the North.

Migrants' Political Identity

Migrants' experiences in the South and the conditions they faced when they arrived in the North contributed to their political identity. As described above, many of them believed that it was important to exercise their right to vote. In part, this belief stemmed from the fact that they had been excluded from politics in their places of origin. In addition to influencing their participation, location also shaped migrants' first party affiliations: they usually aligned with the dominant political machines in their new cities. Where there was a strong Democratic presence (in such cities as New York and Chicago); Black migrants participated as Democrats; in places where the Republican Party was dominant (such as Philadelphia), Black migrants often participated as Republicans. In terms of policy, many migrants were concerned with ending discrimination in schools, housing, and accommodations. Additional policy concerns varied from state to state, which I discuss in later chapters.

What we can learn about migrants on the basis of their origins in different parts of the South is limited in two ways. First, the Great Migration occurred in stages for many people. Like Cora Brown's family, many migrants left rural areas to live in southern urban areas before going north. It would be tremendously difficult to disaggregate truly "urban southerners" from those who were new to or passing through the urban South. Second, to know how people from different areas within the South behaved, we would need data about the localities the migrants left. Although the Census provides aggregate data about the states of origin for migrants, it does not provide data about the migrants' local areas of departure. Where the Census does include individual-level, point-of-departure data about migrants—in the form of a question about where they lived five years ago—it does not include political data. In other words, even when we know where migrants came from, we cannot know how they later participated in politics.

Black Voters as the Potential Balance of Power in Elections

My position is that politicians' and parties' *beliefs* about a unified, unattached voting bloc—a Black balance of power (BOP)—better explain politicians' behavior than the Black population's actual vote. I interrogate my assumption in two ways. First, I conduct content analysis of local newspapers for the period. I search for statements from Black and white politicians about their perceptions of the importance of Black voters in politics. The quoted language from politicians in public statements and in Black and mainstream newspapers make it clear that white political elites did believe that Black voters were important to their political success. Second, I construct a BOP estimate for each of the cities. This BOP calculation provides another way for readers to consider what white politicians believed about Black voting potential during this period. In short, the conclusion—that mayoral candidates changed their behavior to win Black support—follows from the politicians' beliefs about the importance of Black voters, not from the migrants' voting or data.

In instances where party factions or the electorate is split, Black voters sometimes had an exceptional ability to influence the outcome of elections. Black and white leaders, intellectual and political, were aware of their position as the BOP in elections as early as Reconstruction. In the 1886 pamphlet "Negro in Politics," T. Thomas Fortune argues for the political independence of Black people on the grounds that the Republican Party had repeatedly proven itself unworthy of support from Black voters. Further, he asserts that Black people should think about politics only after considering the needs of the race: "race first; then party."[16]

Fortune was among the first Black writers to describe Black voters as a potential BOP in elections; eventually, others would follow. W. E. B. Du Bois would go on to make the same kinds of arguments. Noteworthy is Du Bois's statement for *The Nation* magazine in 1920 about Black voters as the BOP. In it, Du Bois argues that Black voters easily held the balance of power in at least four states—Illinois, Michigan, Indiana, and Kentucky—

because of the large number of Black migrants of voting age. Further, he suggests that Black voters may have been ripe for defection from the Republican Party because it had lost favor with Black Americans during the Howard Taft and Theodore Roosevelt presidential administrations.[17] Du Bois also describes the BOP concept in the pages of the National Association for the Advancement of Colored People's (NAACP's) *Crisis Magazine*. Other writers during the time would take the idea of a Black BOP to be true and include it in their analyses of Black politics.[18]

The most extensive work on Black voters as the BOP would come from Henry Lee Moon, in his 1948 book, *Balance of Power: The Negro Vote*. Because of his work at the NAACP, Moon refers to the Black population as the BOP as a way to persuade political parties and candidates that the Black population should be a top priority in parties' strategies. Further, he suggests that parties should change their positions to appease this very important group of voters. He calculates the BOP for the presidential elections of 1940 and 1944 to argue that Black voters should be an important political consideration of presidential candidates.

Political observers outside the NAACP would also argue that Black voters were the BOP. For example, in a *Collier's* article about the 1956 election, Theodore White describes the importance of the Black vote in terms of Black voters' placement in big cities with large Electoral College (EC) delegations:

> What suddenly draws all political attention to the Negroes in 1956, however, is their phenomenal concentration in the queen cities of five of the biggest voting states of the country: New York, California, Pennsylvania, Illinois and Michigan. These states cast 156 electoral votes, or just 110 short of a Presidential majority. And in the great cities of these states, the Negro population percentage runs from a high of 21 percent in Philadelphia (Mayor Richardson Dilworth unofficially sets it higher, at 25 percent) through 19 percent in Detroit, 17 percent in Chicago, 11 percent (excluding Puerto Ricans, who represent another 6 percent) in New York, 11 percent in Los Angeles.[19]

The Black population was particularly important during the post–World War II period because of their locations and because many of them were entering the political world as new participants.

But some scholars have found the BOP concept wanting in a couple of ways. As presented by Moon and others, the white population of an area must be relatively split between the Democratic and Republican parties for the Black vote to be important in elections. Chuck Stone (1970) argues that this understanding of Black participation in politics is problematic because it fails to acknowledge an alternative where the white population is large and unified on issues. In these instances, Black voters' participation is inconsequential because there are not enough Black votes to affect the outcome of the election. Ronald Walters's (1988) critique of the concept stems from his view that Black voters were not actually politically independent. Walters's theory of dependent-independent leverage asserts that Black voters were captured by and dependent on the Democratic Party. As a result, they could not participate in the voting behavior necessary for the BOP concept to work because they generally had been unwilling to vote for Republicans.[20] Other concerns are methodological, which I discuss further in the following section.

These critiques of the BOP concept are valuable contributions to the literature. However, during the Great Migration years, the dominant way for political elites to consider engagement with Black voters was most often to question whether they were the BOP in elections. If they were not thinking about Black voters as the BOP outright, political elites may have been thinking about Black voters as part of a coalition of voters rather than as a simple BOP. I use the BOP framework because my aim is to describe how politicians and political parties made decisions about their interactions with Black voters. I contend that candidates were behaving based on their beliefs about Black voters as a potential source of votes and powerful coalition partners.

Another reason for my using the BOP framework is to examine the idea in a different context. This book's focus is politics at the state and local levels.[21] Earlier works on the BOP concept—

those that support and those that critique it—have presidential campaigns as their focus. It does not automatically follow that the pitfalls of this theory, as articulated by Stone and Walters, extend to the study of state and local politics. State and local governments are different because of the smaller numbers of votes needed to win election to office and because of potential differences in citizens' expressions of partisanship at these levels. Therefore, observing this theory at the local level is worthwhile.

Calculating the Balance of Power in Local Politics

In part, my argument is built on the assumption that parties and candidates are more attentive to groups whose votes they perceive as the most consequential in elections. One of the goals of this book is to understand whether the conventional wisdom of Moon (1948) and others about Black voters as the BOP is generalizable beyond the elections he analyzes in his text. Specifically, I examine whether Black voters might have been the BOP in subnational elections. The next step is attempting to determine whether Moon and others are correct in their assertion that parties would have been overly concerned with pleasing Black voters because their participation was potentially crucial to their ability to win elections. In other words, I question whether politicians and parties were correct in the assumptions that led to their changing their behavior to accommodate Black interests when they believed that the Black voting bloc might be the BOP. To be clear, whether political elites *believed* that Black voters were the BOP was most important to their decision making. I include the BOP calculations to provide the reader with a sense of the electoral calculations that politicians and parties would have been making during the period.

To determine how often Black voters could have been the BOP during the period of interest, I construct a BOP estimate for every mayoral election in the three cities from 1915 to 1965. Data about the exact number of Black voters registered in states and localities are unavailable before 1965.[22] Therefore, I use the U.S. Census's *Detailed Characteristics of the Population* from

1910 to 1960 to construct a population data set for Black voters in each state from 1915 to 1965. To estimate the number of Black residents who could formally participate in politics—hereafter referred to as the Black voting age population (BVAP)—I include all people classified as Negro and older than age twenty.[23] I gather the same information for the total number of voters in the population, regardless of race—hereafter referred to as the total voting age population (TVAP).

I adapt Moon's formula to determine the BOP for Detroit, New York, and Chicago mayoral elections from 1915 to 1965. I classify Black voters as the BOP in a given election when the BVAP is equal to or greater than the margin of victory in an election. In short, Black voters are the BOP if the number of Black people in the total voting age population is greater than the margin of victory in an election.[24] Following Moon, to get the numerical margin, I add the actual number of votes for Democrats to the actual number of votes for Republicans. Then, I divide the total of the actual vote counts by two. The result of the first two steps is the total number of votes needed to attain exactly half of the vote of the major parties. Because candidates must attain a majority of the vote plus one (1) vote, I add one (1) to the sum of Democratic and Republican votes. Finally, I subtract the number of Republican votes. The result is a numerical margin by which the Democratic Party wins the election. A negative output represents the numerical margin by which the Republican Party wins the election:

Black Voters = BOP if
BVAP > Numerical Margin[25]

To simulate normal participation patterns in elections, I consider whether Black voters' position as the BOP persists without 100 percent involvement from the BVAP. I compare (a) the TVAP to the entire BVAP, (b) two-thirds of the BVAP, and (c) half of the BVAP. The rationale behind these numbers is threefold. First, analyzing a smaller portion of the population than the total allows for analysis of imperfect data about the number of Black people in a city who were registered to vote and/or turned out to vote. Second, I want to account for the process of voter registration. I estimate the number of persons who are registered to vote in the BVAP at 67 percent. Third, I want to account for the fact that fewer than the total number of registered voters turn out to the polls on Election Day. I analyze the BVAP at 50 percent to represent a more likely turnout scenario.

Although we might expect different rates of voting among Black people of this period because of the history of disenfranchisement, migrants to northern cities were more likely to register to vote than counterparts of their race who were already living in the North or white citizens who lived in the North (Gosnell 1967; Gregory 2006; Wilson 1960). For example, William Grimshaw (1992: 53) writes of Black voters in Chicago during the 1944 presidential election, "Black turnout increased by 4 percent, from an already extraordinarily high 91 percent in 1940 to a phenomenal 95 percent." Considering this account, my estimate of 50 percent is conservative. However, I choose this number to acknowledge that Chicago's registration and participation are frequently described as an anomaly and because similar information is not available for all the electoral contests under consideration.

From 1915 to 1965, fifty mayoral elections occurred in the three cities under consideration here. Black voters' standing as the BOP varied by city over time. Overall, with the BVAP at 100 percent, Black voters could have been the BOP in thirty-one elections during the period, or 62 percent of the time. With the estimate at 67 percent, Black voters could have been the BOP in twenty-two of the elections (44 percent). Finally, with the BVAP at 50 percent, Black voters could have been the BOP in seventeen elections (34 percent). For the most part, the likelihood that Black voters were the BOP in local elections was greater in the later part of the period, after the number of Black people in the population had increased. This finding is intuitive because the overall number of Black people in the North was greater in 1965 than it was in 1915. Further, the percentage of Black people residing inside city limits increased exponentially, as Black migration to northern cities coincided with white migration to suburbs.

Ability to Affect Electoral Outcomes

The margin of victory is not the only important part of understanding how groups of voters affect elections. Parties must also consider that obtaining an electoral majority will require support from more than one group. Therefore, any group that is a sizable portion of the margin of victory should be important to a party for its potential to add to the party's win number—even if the size of that group is not enough to win or change the outcome of the election outright. Parties are looking for enough voters to get to their "win number" and understand that this strategy means drawing on more than one group of people. A party does not need the entire vote of a group for that group to have a positive, important impact on an election. In determining whether a group was the BOP, the margin of victory is important because it tells us how many votes could change the outcome of the election.

Beyond the sheer size of a group, parties must also consider the costs and benefits of constructing a new coalition. A party's strategy—either to stay the same or to court new groups—has consequences. If a party remains the same, it may forgo the benefits of incorporating a new group. However, adding new members to the group's existing coalition might create tension or resistance among current coalition members. Parties had to weigh the costs and benefits of incorporating Black voters into their coalitions. For Black voters to be worth the risks to a candidate or a party in the North—and to positively affect the party's electoral calculus—enough of them needed to be in an area to reasonably and substantially contribute to the party's win number or to the construction of a viable electoral majority. I assume that parties and candidates were particularly concerned with trying to meet the needs of Black voters in cities when those voters had the ability to swing elections.

Problems with Migrant Voter Data, 1915–1965

I have long been curious about migrant voter data, especially what these data might teach us about the evolution of Black voters' party affiliations. The dominant narrative is that Black voters converted from the Republican Party to the Democratic Party, beginning during the New Deal and finishing by the 1964 presidential election. However, I argue here that part of the change in Black voters' party affiliations should also be described as mobilization and attributed to Democrats' efforts to engage the influx of northern Black voters. In an attempt to understand the potential for mobilization as an explanation for party change for a different project, I tried to measure change in the number of Black Democrats and Republicans in Chicago from 1935 to 1965. I encountered a few challenges in the attempt to track Black voting behavior between 1915 and 1965.

First, most historical voter registration data for the period do not include information about the races of the registrants. Therefore, I attempted to estimate Black voters' party affiliations in Chicago by examining their aggregate voting patterns. I focused on precinct- and ward-level data for two historically Black neighborhoods in Chicago—University of Chicago Community Areas 38 and 40 (Grand Boulevard and Washington Park, respectively)—because their populations were more than 95 percent Black throughout the entire period of interest. Additionally, unlike precincts and wards, the boundaries of the University of Chicago Community Areas remained the same across the entire period.

To see how Black voters behaved, I wanted to observe changes in the precincts over time. The second challenge was tracking precinct-level voting patterns in the Black community for more than one election. Collecting the data to understand Black voting trends requires substantial effort and coordination with the Chicago Board of Elections (BOE) staff. At least two issues remained as serious challenges for the aforementioned study and this book, by extension. First, the Chicago BOE's policies have evolved such that researchers are not allowed to sort through historical records to organize data for themselves; the information must be furnished by BOE staff. The BOE staff was unable to match the precincts to the census tracts associated with Community Areas 38 and 40 for many of the elections from 1935 to 1965.

Second, the few precincts I was able to observe in the available data changed frequently—after almost every election. The wards changed less often, every ten years, as politicians sought to redraw the lines for fair distribution of the population or for their own personal gain. These frequent changes make it nearly impossible to compare precinct- or ward-level Black voting patterns across decades, which would be necessary to comment on Black voting behavior over both waves of the Great Migration. The result is that I have reliable and consistent precinct-level data for a very small number of the elections during the period. In short, the data do not lend themselves to comparison across elections for the entire period.

Although I do not analyze individual-level voting data in this book, I do support my central claims about Democratic politicians' beliefs and interactions with Black voters in two other ways. For statements from the politicians themselves, I draw on accounts of the period from Black and mainstream newspapers in each of the cities. For additional information about politicians' interactions with Black communities, I rely on the wealth of literature about local politics in each of the cities.

Conclusion

This chapter describes the Great Migration as an important consideration in the debates about change in American political parties by asserting that parties and politicians were likely to respond to the increase in Black voters as a function of their desire to retain office. I also describe the increase in the number of Black elected officials in northern legislatures and city councils as an important by-product of the Great Migration. The chapter also situates the Great Migration in the compositional effects literature. Further, I contribute to the literature on contextual effects by asserting that existing descriptions of political immunization should consider the disenfranchisement that Black Americans suffered.

As Black people flooded into northern cities during the Great Migration, they changed local politics by forcing parties to incorporate them into electoral calculations or to devise strategies to keep them out. For at least three reasons, it is important to consider how change occurred in political parties' interactions with Black voters at the subnational level. First, local government is the point of entry into politics for most groups. Second, because of their smaller units of competition, groups may influence outcomes in subnational elections with more ease than in national elections. Third, trends in subnational elections sometimes shape later national party responses to groups on other issues.

I argue that migrants' impact on local parties, through mayoral candidates, varied on the basis of two factors: (1) the interaction of the spatial distribution of Black people and the rules for election to office and (2) the degree of party competition. Local parties were more concerned with campaigning to and meeting the needs of Black voters in cities with racially segregated neighborhoods and small, ward-based local electoral systems. During the period of interest, local competition for political power occurred in several ways: parties competed against each other in general elections; parties competed internally, through factions, in primary election battles; or interest groups worked in coalitions to influence elections.

Black voters were especially impactful in cities with a high degree of competition between parties or party factions, which sometimes led parties and candidates to campaign to win Black votes in a positive manner. In these situations, Black voters—voting as a bloc—could have been the deciding factor in elections where the overall electorate was split. I assume that parties were particularly concerned with meeting the demands of any group of voters that had, or appeared to have, this kind of BOP in party power struggles. In other words, Black voters might have been considered especially important coalition partners in instances where party factions were divided in their attempt to gain control of cities.

In the chapters that follow, I explain migrants' interactions with politics in each of the cities in two ways. First, I focus on mayoral candidates' interactions with Black voters from 1915 to 1965 to describe their approach to reaching Black voters or attempting to exclude them. I describe the electoral results in terms of support for the Black community. I find that political candidates were thoughtful about and responsive to Black voters in the electorate. In some instances, their responses were positive; in others, their responses were negative.

Second, I examine the political involvement and policy concerns of Black elected officials, paying specific attention to migrants' political participation. More than half of the Black elected officials were migrants. Most of the elected officials, regardless of their migration status, were concerned about similar issues. They introduced legislation to end discrimination in various parts of Black life. In some instances, they were specifically concerned with issues related to migration and the living conditions of migrants. They used their positions to bring attention to issues of concern to their Black constituents. Therefore, consideration of the Great Migration is essential to understanding politics in northern cities from 1915 to 1965.

2

Black Migration in American History

In Black American culture, one of the most common ways to get to know someone is to ask: "Where are your people from?" Often without the inquisitor's conscious knowledge, the question presupposes a significant move in the course of the average Black person's family history. In the South, responses may indicate that some member of the family left a rural area in favor of a southern city or moved north at some point and later chose to return to the South. In the North, responses generally point southward. For example, in Chicago and Detroit, the answer is frequently Louisiana, Mississippi, or Alabama. For people from New York, the answer is often Florida, Georgia, or South Carolina. Without calling it by name, the question "Where are your people from?" acknowledges that the Great Migration looms large in most African American family histories.

The Great Migration was one of the largest movements of the population in American history. It was larger than the preceding California gold rush and dust bowl migrations combined (Wilkerson 2010: 10). After settlers discovered gold in 1848, the nonnative population of California grew from fewer than one thousand people to one hundred thousand over the course of two years. In the 1930s, following the Great Depression, California's population experienced another boom. The dust bowl migration drew nearly three million Americans from Oklahoma, Texas, Arkansas, and Missouri to California. By contrast, six and a half million Black Americans would leave the South over the course of the Great Migration, changing the composition of American cities and states in the North and the South.[1] In the first wave of the migration, "it is conservatively estimated that over 400,000 left in the two-year period, 1916–1918. They left at an average rate of over 16,000 per month, 500 per day" (Marks 1989: 1). Far more people moved in the second wave of the migration, with an estimated four and a half million migrants leaving the South after 1940.

Over the course of the twentieth century, the number of Black people living outside the South increased dramatically as they moved to large, industrial cities. Whereas their numbers in the North had been negligible at the beginning of the century, nearly half of the Black population in the United States was living outside the South by the end of the migration in 1970. This mass exodus of Black people would eventually change the American demographic landscape and help facilitate one of the most profound developments in American history, the civil rights movement.

The Great Migration was one in a series of Black migrations that have occurred over the history of Africans in America. As soon as they arrived on the shores of the North American continent, Black Americans were moving. These earlier movements would eventually shape the Great Migration. In the first part of this chapter, I briefly describe earlier Black migrations. Then, I turn my attention to the Great Migration to explain how it occurred, Black Americans' motivation for leaving the South, and the average profile of Black migrants. Last, I lay the foundation for Chapters 3–5 by describing twentieth-century Black migrants as potential political participants. I chart the growth of the Black voting age population (BVAP) in Detroit, New York, and Chicago and describe how it created the potential for Black voters to influence politics.

History of Black Migration in America

Migration of Black people in America has occurred voluntarily and involuntarily since the first Africans came to the North American continent in the 1500s. A free African named Juan Garrido was with Juan Ponce de León when he arrived in Florida in 1513. The first large group of Africans came to America from Hispaniola in 1526 (Johnson and Campbell 1981). The transatlantic and transcontinental passages were the two major forced migrations that preceded the Great Migration (Berlin 2010). Although they are discussed less frequently, voluntary migrations occurred alongside these movements (LaRoche 2014: 180). I begin this section by describing the involuntary migrations of the Atlantic and transcontinental slave trades. Next, I discuss voluntary movements, including migration as unconnected to larger movements and migration that engaged broader, organized communities. Finally, I describe the largest Black migration in America—the Great Migration.[2]

Involuntary Migration

Europeans forced the migration of approximately five hundred thousand African people from their continent's shores to North America. Millions more went to the Caribbean and Latin America. The Atlantic slave trade lasted until 1808, more than thirty years after America's own fight for freedom in the Revolutionary War (Wood 2000: 71).[3] Black people were the foundation of the plantation economy. They planted crops, constructed buildings, maintained homes, and cared for their oppressors' children.

While British colonists in America were fighting for their freedom, they facilitated the continued bondage and forced migration of Black people. Some enslaved people were forced to move to the North as their owners moved. Many others remained enslaved in the mid-Atlantic and fought alongside their masters for freedom from Great Britain (Cahill 1999). During the war years, some enslaved people escaped to Canada in individual attempts to secure their freedom. Migration to Canada continued when the war was over, as many Black enslaved people left for Nova Scotia with the British soldiers who were leaving the United States. Some continued their migration beyond Canada, choosing to live in Great Britain or Sierra Leone (LaRoche 2014: 105).

Forced Black migration continued after America outlawed the transatlantic slave trade. At the beginning of the slave trade, such mid-Atlantic states as Delaware, Maryland, and Virginia were the primary destination for and location of imported enslaved people. During the transcontinental trade, the center of slavery shifted. Enslaved people would be moved south and west through regularized channels: "Its terminals—Alexandria, Baltimore, Richmond, Norfolk, and Washington at one end and Natchez, New Orleans, and Vicksburg at the other—became infamous" (Berlin 2010: 103). By the 1830s, Alabama and Mississippi were the most likely destinations for enslaved people moving involuntarily within the United States. Eventually, these states had Black populations that exceeded their white populations. Later, Mississippi and Alabama would be a primary point of origin for participants in the Great Migration (Gregory 2006: 33).

Voluntary Migration

Not all Black migration was forced. Enslaved Africans left the homes of their oppressors in numbers small and large. It is difficult to know the exact number of people who migrated by running away and attempting to reach nonslave states because most went in unceremonious fashion, on relatively uncoordinated trips:

> Lack of agreement on the total number of escapees in the United States hampers accurate estimations. Some historians have claimed the number hovered near 40,000. Others think it more probable "that somewhere between 40,000 and 100,000 African Americans . . . found freedom." (LaRoche 2014: 104)

Early voluntary movements of Black people out of the South were small. Younger men, traveling alone, were most likely to leave. When freedom seekers did travel with others, their groups were very small in size. A study of advertisements seeking the return of South Carolina runaways found that "most (70 percent) of the advertised groups only included two slaves" (M. Johnson 1981: 420).[4] Migration via running away would evolve over time as governments created laws at different levels to deter the practice and as groups of people worked together to increase the number of enslaved people reaching freedom.

The U.S. government passed numerous laws to protect African slavery. The laws began by binding slavery to race instead of debt or service, which had been the practice at the earliest parts of the nation's history. Eventually, laws evolved to specify that enslaved Africans' unfree status was permanent and contingent on the will of white owners of enslaved people. Their classification as such persisted, even if they were able to earn enough money to buy their freedom or to relocate to free states and territories. Further, the laws evolved to specify that the children of enslaved people were subject to slavery as a condition of their birth. In some communities, white Americans refused to adhere to the government's declaration that slavery was a semipermanent state. In these places, an enslaved person was considered free if she or he made it to free soil. A few northern communities went as far as physically fighting southerners who sought to forcibly remove Black people from their jurisdictions (Blackett 2013: 44).

The Fugitive Slave Law of 1850 pushed for the protection of slavery in new ways by going beyond the usual practice of allowing payment to slave catchers for returned enslaved people: it required white people to face legal punishment if they did not return Black freedom seekers to slavery (LaRoche 2014: 120). This law put Black people throughout the nation at risk. Those who had been born free or had otherwise earned their freedom could be captured and sent south with little consequence. In response to this legislation, many Black people who were already living outside the South went farther north into Canada. Additionally, the number of Black people attempting to flee the South grew tremendously and led to "a peak in travel on the Underground Railroad" around 1850 (Bontemps and Conroy 1966: 3).

While some Black people fled slavery in small, independent groups, many others left as part of larger movements of groups and through assistance from abolitionists. The Underground Railroad was the most well-known movement of enslaved people out of the South. It was established in the 1840s as a network of individuals, churches, and other organizations working together to facilitate passage to the North. The Underground Railroad's most well-known "conductor," Harriet Tubman, led the migration of three hundred enslaved people to the North from 1849 to 1860 (Ciment 2007). Altogether, the Underground Railroad was responsible for the migration of approximately one hundred thousand people.

The end of slavery and the ensuing emancipation marked another chapter in the story of voluntary Black migration. Formerly enslaved people moved to look for loved ones, to figure out how to take care of themselves, and just because they could in some instances (Painter 1977). But lack of resources limited the kinds of migration open to formerly enslaved Africans. Therefore, many Black people remained in the South. Some moved from very rural farms into southern cities. Others with the means to do so moved north (Goodwin 1990: 1).

Migration to Kansas and Kansas Fever of 1879

After emancipation, three major strands of thought described Black Americans' ideas about migration: (1) Black people should remain in the South and fight to make it hospitable for Black people; (2) Black people should immigrate to other nations, including Sierra Leone, Liberia, and Haiti; and (3) Black people should migrate northward within the United States because it was a more feasible move for many people. The two major post-Reconstruction migrations of Black Americans—the Kansas Fever Movement and the Kansas Exodus of 1879, or Exoduster Movement—grew out of these debates.

The state of Kansas was a frequent consideration among Black Americans in discussions about moving within the United States. They were attracted to Kansas because it was accessible. Further, it was a free state. Black southerners were especially attracted to the struggle that had occurred in the state over its free status:

> For Afro-American migrants, Kansas represented something that Nebraska and the Dakotas did not. To make Kansas a Free State, blood flowed freely during the 1850s. It was the quintessential Free State, the land of John Brown, "a free state in which a colored man can enjoy his freedom." He could prosper under his own vine and fig tree and watch his children grow up free and educated. (Painter 1977: 159)

In 1874 and 1875, Black people began going to Kansas from Tennessee in a seemingly spontaneous movement that was based on rumors of free transportation and government support through land allotments and farming supplies. Such people as Benjamin "Pap" Singleton, who were motivated by personal business interests, helped them along in their movement. A Tennessee native, Singleton first encouraged Black families—mostly from South Carolina and Georgia—to move to Tennessee. When it became clear that investment in Tennessee farms would be tremendously difficult, Singleton began to suggest that Black people buy land and settle in Kansas (Painter 1977: 115).

The Kansas Exodus of 1879—the Exoduster Movement—was a planned migration to Kansas in reaction to the abandonment of Reconstruction. When Reconstruction ended, southern Democrats led the charge to repeal its gains by enshrining discrimination into law during a period they called "redemption." Black people, on the other hand, called the post-Reconstruction era "the Nadir." In some Black communities, the end of Reconstruction's inclusive policies led to debate about whether they should leave the South en masse. Between the two movements, approximately twenty-six thousand additional Black people moved to

Kansas from various parts of the central South—mostly Louisiana, Mississippi, Texas, and Tennessee (Painter 1977). Some migrants opted to go even farther to New York, New Jersey, and Pennsylvania. Approximately thirty thousand people migrated to mid-Atlantic states, with about half of them settling in Pennsylvania (Johnson and Campbell 1981).

These migrations were important to the spatial placement of Black people in America. By 1910, Black Americans lived in more places than ever. Although many faced resource challenges that contributed to their decisions to remain in the South, some left to try life in the North. But these early movements of Black Americans paled in comparison to what would occur later in the twentieth century. In the rest of this chapter, I describe the largest migration—the Great Migration—in terms of its causes, participants, and potential to influence American politics.

The Great Migration

Scholars debate the exact start and end of the Great Migration. However, most agree that migration occurred in two waves, as prompted by world wars and changes in the agricultural economy (Gregory 2006; Johnson and Campbell 1981; Scott 1920; Spear 1967). The first wave began around 1915, as northern industrial labor agents—who offered to pay moving expenses and help migrants find accommodations in the North—entered the state of Florida, looking for individuals who were willing to relocate to Pennsylvania for work (Johnson and Campbell 1981: 72; Scott 1920: 38). Once it became clear to Black southerners that opportunities for work were available outside the South, they started moving on their own, and the use of labor agents decreased.

In the late 1920s and early 1930s, the Great Depression slowed the migration to half its previous pace as opportunities for work disappeared (Trotter 1991: 10):

> Despite high unemployment, nearly 300,000 blacks moved out of the South during the 1930s, partly because new public assistance programs helped mitigate the im-

> pact of declining employment in the private sector. (Trotter 1991: 11)

The number of people going north increased again after the start of America's involvement in World War II. The second wave of the Great Migration began in the 1940s and lasted through the 1960s. Of the six and a half million Black people who left the South, five million of them left after 1940 (Lemann 1992). Although sociologists and historians tend to focus on the first wave of migration, the second wave is equally important and warrants consideration because it involved a much larger portion of the population. Further, pertaining to the study of politics, the second wave of the migration was when Black communities became large enough to influence politics.

How Did They Migrate?

The first stop on a migrant's journey northward was often an urban area in the South, such as Memphis, Birmingham, Jacksonville, or Atlanta (Gregory 2006; Marks 1989: 3). Although the economic opportunities in urban areas of the South were better than those in the rural areas, they could not compete with the promises of the North. Migrants who chose to go farther north usually moved up in parallel streams, depicted in Figure 2.1 (Ciment 2007; Gregory 2006; Johnson and Campbell 1981; Scott 1920). Migrants leaving Florida, Georgia, and the Carolinas went to states along the mid-Atlantic and the East Coasts. Many settled in Pennsylvania (Philadelphia and Pittsburgh), New York (New York City and Buffalo), and New Jersey (Newark, Paterson, and Jersey City). Those leaving parts of the South that were farther inland migrated to cities that were also farther inland. The residents of Mississippi, Alabama, and Tennessee often went to Illinois (Chicago and East St. Louis), Missouri (St. Louis), Ohio (Cleveland), and Michigan (Detroit). Migrants who lived in Louisiana, Oklahoma, Texas, and Arkansas were more likely to relocate to California[5] (Los Angeles, Oakland, and Richmond) (Gregory 2006; Johnson and Campbell 1981: 116; Scott 1920: 55).

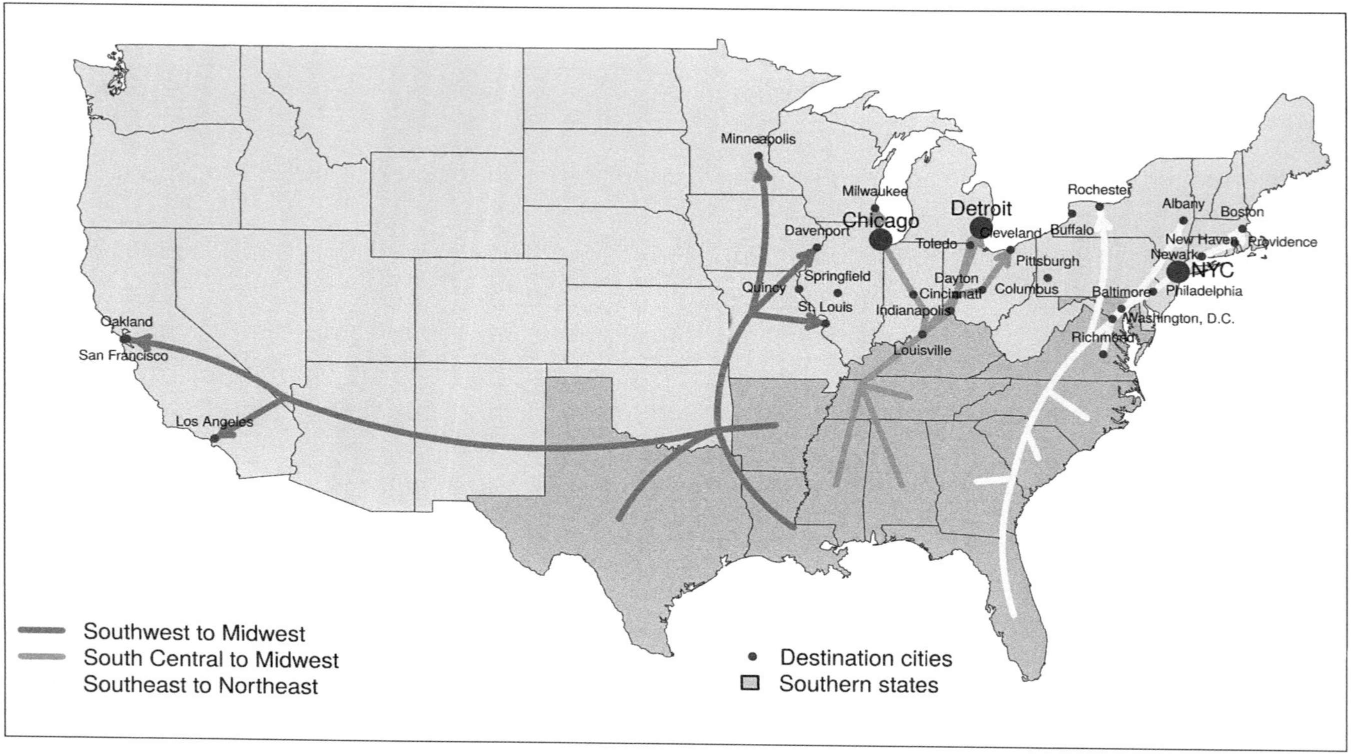

Figure 2.1. Great migration streams. (Courtesy of Candy Martinez.)

Migrants were often limited in their ability to move by discrimination in the provision of transportation services and their lack of resources. In the early stages of the Great Migration, travel by boat and train were popular. Travel by automobile increased in the later years. The parallel streams reflected migrants' reliance on accessible and affordable modes of transportation.

Who Led the Migration?

Individual leaders emerged in the migrations that preceded the Great Migration. For example, we think of Harriet Tubman in connection with movements during slavery and Pap Singleton as associated with migration to Kansas. However, it is difficult to point to a singular person as the leader of the Great Migration. The decision to go north was mostly individual, made by a young person who decided to try making it on her own or made by a husband and wife who decided one of them would go north and send for the rest of the family later (Marks 1989; Scott 1920). Because no one authoritative source encouraged migrants to leave the South, migration scholars have often described the Great Migration as a leaderless movement (Painter 1977; Wilkerson 2010).

Although it had no singular leader, the migration was not totally without influence from individuals, groups, and organizations. Migration clubs in the South worked to facilitate passage into the North. These clubs included groups of people who worked together to travel north by negotiating collective travel rates and lodging in the new city (Grossman 1989: 66). Black professionals who wanted to go north understood the importance of facilitating the movement of their networks. They would have been among the class of people encouraging others to leave the South. On the other geographic side of the migration, some people worked to draw more Black people out of the South so they could build communities.

Black media outlets, especially a newspaper called the *Chicago Defender* (the *Defender*), were important thought leaders on issues related to the migration. The *Defender* played a critical role in stirring excitement and disseminating information about migration to the North. Circulated and read throughout Black America—including the South—the paper was often a very aggressive advocate for Black migration. For example, the *Defender* called for a "Great Northern Drive" to occur on May 15, 1917, and encouraged people considering a move to go north on that date (Scott 1920). Hundreds of people wrote to the newspaper, seeking details about the mass movement. The result of the paper's marketing campaign was that large numbers of people did arrive in the North around the paper's suggested move date.

The *Defender* was also a source of practical information for potential migrants. Black southerners wrote to the *Defender* for advice about where they might be able to work or live. An example of a typical letter from a migrant writing for help with employment and lodging in 1917 follows:

> Dear Sir: In reading a copy of *The Chicago Defender* . . . if I get in touch with you, you would assist me in getting employment. I am not employed. I [live on] the Florida East coast. R. R. Service [or] road way department [. . .] anything in working line myself [and] friends would be more than glad to do so and would highly appreciate it the very best we can advise where we can get work to do, fairly good wages. [A]lso is it possible that we could get transportation to the destination. We are working men with families. Please answer at once. I am your esteem. We are not particular about the electric lights and all I want is fairly good wages and steady work. Jacksonville, Florida, 4-25-17. (Goodwin 1990: 13)

Word of mouth and family networks were important in spreading the word about and stimulating migration. The best advertisements for life in the North were shared through letters from those who were already gone, recruitment ads from employers, and organizations seeking to help migrants' transition. Through these forms of correspondence, migrants described how they were able to find work, what their living conditions were like, and how northerners treated them (Marks 1989: 25; Scott 1920: 34). Churches, civic organizations, and barbershops and beauty salons in the South were hotbeds of conversation and discussion about whether it was a good idea to move.

People were divided on the issue of migration, which meant that migrants had to manage conflicting sources of information. The flip side of working to build community in the North was the loss of communities in the South. When Black populations dwindled in the South, Black pastors lost congregations, doctors lost patients, and lawyers lost potential clients. In some instances, moving meant defying the advice of community leaders in the South, who encouraged people to remain in the region and wait for conditions to improve (Grossman 1989: 64). These leaders advocated staying near family and maintaining southern Black communities. Still others argued that migration was necessary for progress of the race (Goodwin 1990; Scott 1920).

Who Migrated?

Many young adults left the South in search of work and liberty. Highly educated Black people were among the most likely to move. Migration of the so-called talented tenth—which included the college-educated or highly skilled segment of the Black population—demonstrates this point (Woodson 1970: 147). Whereas only 6 percent of the Black population who remained in the South had high school diplomas, 22 percent of the participants in the Great Migration reported that they had finished high school (Gregory 2006: 31). Many young Black people with great academic potential were forced to attend private northern colleges because southern states denied Black students access to their schools. Rather than integrate, southern states paid Black students to study in the North. Some of the young people who were paid to prevent integration by studying elsewhere never returned to the South. Others, such as Michigan state senator Cora Brown, who is mentioned in this book's Introduction, left the North to attend historically Black colleges and universities (HBCUs) but returned to northern cities upon graduation. Similarly, some Black southerners attended HBCUs in the South and decided to relocate to the North when they graduated. Soldiers returning from World War II migrated in a similar pattern. After military service, many who were born in the South found it difficult to return to their inferior "place" in the southern social system and chose to live in the North.

Gender and marital status also influenced migration patterns (White et al. 2005). In the first wave of the Great Migration, men were more likely to move than women (Marks 1989: 36). However, the second wave was proportionately more female (Gregory 2006; Johnson and Campbell 1981). Women actively supported the entire migration even when they themselves could not move. They led families while male migrants were away. For example, they took jobs as domestic workers to provide financial support. They also frequently took responsibility for younger members of their extended families in cases where two parents decided to move and send for children later.[6]

Single men and married couples were more likely to choose a diverse set of destinations. They might move to areas outside major cities or to rural areas in the North. On the other hand, unmarried women were more likely to choose destinations in metropolitan centers. Cities provided better opportunities for women to support themselves independent of attachment to men. Therefore, greater numbers of them chose such places as Chicago instead of Evanston or Philadelphia instead of Allentown. There was also some regional variation in the population of movers based on the predominant industry. Men were disproportionately represented in the population of movers to the Midwest because they took jobs in factories. Women, who were more likely to take positions as domestic workers, were overrepresented in the population of migrants who moved to the Northeast.

Why Migrate?

This work builds on others that assert that economic conditions were the foremost consideration in most southern Black Americans' decisions to move. Further, it adds that social considerations played some part in migrants' decision to go north.[7] Economic conditions throughout the nation, including changes in the farming and war economies, prompted many people to move (Holley 2000; Marks 1989; Scott 1920). At the same time, some movers went north in search of freedom from racial discrimination. They hoped to live in places that were not segregated and would provide equal opportunity for their families.

Great Migration literature describes the economic conditions as push or pull factors. Push factors were negative occurrences that drove migrants out of the South. Critical among these during the early migration was a boll-weevil infestation that destroyed cotton crops and affected the viability of the cotton economy. Even before boll weevils wreaked havoc, Black people had struggled to make a living as they tried to coexist with white landowners as tenant farmers or sharecroppers (Bontemps and Conroy 1966: 159). The infestations of 1915 and 1916 depressed crop prices and dashed what little hope Black sharecroppers might have had for getting landowners to pay them a reasonable wage or share any percentages of farm profits. The advent of the mechanical cotton picker also changed the cotton economy and pushed people to migrate in the second wave. The mechanical cotton picker was the most revolutionary change in the production of cotton since the cotton gin and practically eliminated the need for human labor in the cotton industry during the 1940s. These changes in the economy left Black southerners with few ways to earn a living in the South and pushed them off farms in search of other work. But even without developments in agricultural technology, Black laborers in the South had been considering ways to attain higher wages and better standards of living:

> Most of the migrants were not pushed out by mechanical cotton pickers; they were pulled out in a search for better economic opportunities. . . . [T]hey were trying to escape the hard work and low pay associated with southern cotton fields. (Holley 2000: 283)

World Wars I and II also influenced the nature of the Great Migration. The pull factors included expanded opportunities for employment and the potential for higher wages created by war-era growth in the economy. The wars increased national industrial production overall, creating greater job opportunities in the North. However, during World War I, Black migrants who settled in the North found that employers discriminated against them in terms of hiring, preferring to employ European immigrants instead. As the war continued, the U.S. Congress sought to limit the number and type of people entering the United States from parts of Europe and passed a series of bills in 1917, 1921, and 1924 designed to limit immigration (Hellwig 1981). As a result, the number of Europeans coming to America decreased from nearly 1,000,000 per year to approximately 250,000. For industries, a consequence of these restrictions was an immediate decrease in the number of available white ethnic workers to fill positions in northern factories. The decreased supply of white European workers and the increased demand for products forced businesses to hire minorities and women.[8]

Although the push/pull metaphor in the Great Migration scholarship is traditionally limited to economic considerations, the metaphor could expand to account for social factors that encouraged migration (Grossman 1989: 17; see also Wilkerson 2010: 533–534). There were the civic, educational, and political benefits of living outside the South. In the North, Black people could gain access to substantially sized, upwardly mobile communities of similarly situated individuals. This environment would have been different from most Black communities in the South, including urban areas (Johnson and Campbell 1981: 145). Migration allowed Black people to indulge some of the luxuries of middle-class American life. Although Black Americans experienced major challenges and limits when assimilating outside Black neighborhoods, they could often purchase homes or join and have leadership positions in civic and religious organizations within their northern communities.

Moving to the North also meant better educational opportunities for the children of migrants. Many southern schools lacked resources and maintained abbreviated school calendars so that Black children could work in the fields instead of attending classes during the harvest and planting seasons (Johnson and Campbell 1981: 109):

> Florida school boards, each with its own little fiefdom, had a habit of shutting down the colored schools weeks or months before the school year was supposed to end, blaming the closures on budget shortfalls that for some reason did not affect class time at the white schools. (Wilkerson 2010: 321)

On the contrary, northern schools maintained longer calendars and, in some instances, had compulsory attendance policies (Grossman 1989). The situation in northern schools was by no means perfect. For example, they were frequently overcrowded because districts failed to manage the growth of the migrant population. Some northern school districts were also segregated. However, even with these problems in northern schools, migrants calculated that their children would have access to better educations by living in the North than they would if they remained in the South.[9]

Beyond the economic and social pull factors drawing migrants to the North, some of the reasons for migration were moral—having to do with Black Americans' sense of fairness, justice, and the way they deserved to be treated (Painter 1977; Wilkerson 2010). They wanted equality in access to facilities and public accommodations and hoped their move would bring them a greater degree of freedom from discrimination and violence in their everyday lives (Marks 1989). In short, Black Americans wanted to fully participate in American society and receive all the privileges available to other citizens.

For many Black southerners, motivations for migration included a desire to participate in the political process as voters and office holders. In interviews, many migrants describe a desire to exercise the full rights of American citizenship (Woodson 1970). Voter registration was a chief concern for some of the movers, who held this basic act of citizenship in the highest regard and considered their voter registrations to be badges of honor. Consider this letter from a Hattiesburg, Mississippi, migrant to his friend about the social benefits of moving north:

> I should have been here twenty years ago. I just begin to feel like a man. It's a great deal of pleasure in knowing that you have got some privileges. My children are going to the same school with whites and I don't have to humble to no one. I have registered. Will vote the next election and there isn't any "yes, sir, and no, sir." (Scott 1920: 34)

For the rest of this chapter, I consider migrants through a political lens, as potential participants in the political process through voting and office holding.

Migrants as Potential Voters

The Great Migration is the only instance in American history in which a group of American citizens had to leave their home region to be able to meaningfully participate in the political process. Whereas it was often nearly impossible to vote in the South, Black people faced fewer overt challenges to their participation in the North. In many instances, migrants were immediately eligible for political participation because states in the North had shorter barriers to voting for Black Americans than did the southern states. In some places, political parties might help migrants in the process of political participation. Migrants could—and did—organize themselves to make appeals to political candidates, support campaigns, and even run for elected office. They could register to vote, and they could exercise that right to vote with relative ease on Election Day. When Black people attempted these sorts of activities in the South, they were met with hostilities that decreased the likelihood of their participation.

The population of migrants from the South included an oversample of eligible voters because the average migrant was between the ages of twenty and twenty-five. Further, many of the migrants had characteristics that generally led to a greater likelihood of their participation. For example, as previously described, many of them were involved in social clubs and organizations or attended church services regularly:

> Political participation was important to the migrants, who like many other Americans considered the right to vote central to their status as citizens. In the South the ballot box had symbolized not only racial proscription and white monopoly of formal authority, but also the inextricable relationship between class and racial proscription in the form of the poll tax. (Grossman 1989: 175)

Migrants' citizenship status made them attractive to political parties that sought to register and mobilize voters. The vast majority of migrants were born in the United States and therefore—unlike their European counterparts in northern cities—were already U.S. citizens. This status meant that parties, which were seeking to influence elections by capitalizing on changes in the electorate, could expand their bases by registering the newly arrived Black southerners to vote in the North.

Whereas parties might have to convince voting-age people to change their political behavior or convert from one party to another, migrants were non-immunized voters. They may have come to the North with ideas about political parties, but most of them had never participated in politics before they moved. Therefore, Black southerners may have been more open to overtures from parties—the Democratic Party in particular—because they did not have established records of political participation: "The new citizens are non-immunized: while they may enter the system with a partisan preference, their lack of political experience means their partisan commitment is lower—and their potential political volatility greater—than other citizens" (Andersen 1979: 73).

In Chicago, for example, Democrats met registrants at train

stations or paid visits to their homes shortly after they resettled (Marks 1989; Wilkerson 2010):

> [Democrats] went door-to-door to talk up the New Deal and register people. They asked about kids and jobs and convinced [migrants] that the Democrats in the North were different from those in the South. They printed up party slates and passed out palm cards—political crib notes that would fit in the palm of the hand—so people would know who to vote for when they got inside the booth. (Wilkerson 2010: 304)

But getting involved with northern political processes was not without its obstacles. For example, issues finding stable residences made it difficult for some migrants to meet the eligibility requirements for voter registration. But, overall, the problems of voting in the North paled in comparison to those faced by Black Americans who were attempting to vote in the South.

Although migrants' U.S. citizenship status could be beneficial to local political organizations, their desire to participate in politics was met in some areas with varying levels of resistance that ranged from ignoring the new residents to trying to diminish their influence through vote-busting schemes (Erie 1990). Where parties were well organized, voter registration assistance occasionally came with strings attached, as machines sometimes forced Black people to support specific political parties or face economic retribution. In cities that did not have well-organized local party systems, migrants were sometimes not included in political processes. Yet in spite of all the challenges, Black voter-registration and turnout levels frequently matched those of the white population and were even higher in some instances (Wilson 1960: 39; see also Gosnell 1967; Moon 1948).

Growth of the Black Voting Age Population

The Great Migration led to the potential enfranchisement of millions of Black American citizens who had been unable to

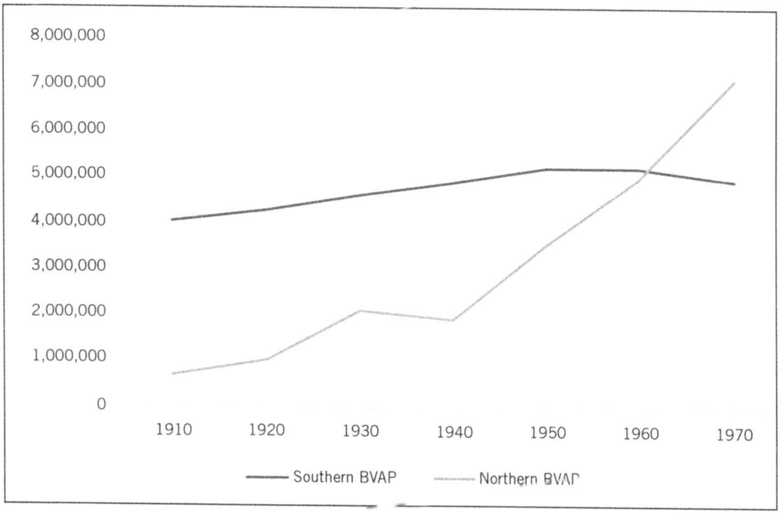

Figure 2.2. Black voting age population, by region, 1910–1970. (Based on U.S. Census, *Detailed Characteristics of the Population, 1910–1970.*)

participate in the political process when they lived in the South. In 1910, given the challenges of participating in politics in the South, less than 20 percent of the Black population may have been able to participate in politics. As Black people left the South during the Great Migration, the number of them who could potentially participate in politics grew exponentially. Approximately 43 percent of them would have been able to participate in 1960.[10] Over the course of the Great Migration, two trends occurred simultaneously in the Black population: (1) the overall BVAP was growing and (2) the distribution of Black people in the regions was changing (see Figure 2.2). In other words, the Black population was growing not only as a percentage of people outside the South but also through natural means.

The migrants' political impact was especially pronounced in the large cities where they settled. Table 2.1 shows how Black voters grew as a percentage of the overall population in three cities: Chicago, Detroit, and New York. In the beginning of the Great Migration, Black populations—and, by extension, Black electorates—were small in these cities. However, by the end of

TABLE 2.1. BLACK PERCENTAGE OF THE TOTAL VOTING AGE POPULATION IN THREE CITIES			
	Detroit	New York	Chicago
1910	2.9%	2.6%	2.9%
1920	8.5%	3.2%	4.8%
1930	8.3%	5.1%	7.7%
1940	9.1%	6.0%	8.0%
1950	16.1%	9.1%	13.0%
1960	25.2%	12.7%	19.6%
1970	38.2%	17.8%	42.0%

Source: U.S. Census, *Detailed Characteristics of the Population, 1910–1970.* Compiled by the author.

the migration, Black people accounted for a considerable segment of many urban electorates.

Conclusion

Black Americans have migrated in America since they first arrived. Their movements were forced and voluntary, happening through individual decisions and in groups. Although different factors influenced migration, a central theme in the movements is Black Americans' attempt to make better lives for themselves economically, socially, and politically. The Great Migration took Black people from a position of nonvoting to voting. The changes were especially pronounced in large states and cities, where migrants were most likely to settle. Therefore, the Great Migration resulted in one of the most politically significant demographic changes in American history. In the next three chapters, I describe migrants' impact on state and local politics in Detroit, New York, and Chicago, respectively.

3

Detroit

Black migrants to Detroit were interested in the economic opportunities the city had to offer. In particular, the automobile industry created the potential for Black workers to earn good wages. Henry Ford pledged to pay workers five dollars per day, regardless of their race. The average Black person in the South had no comparable opportunities. Large numbers of southern migrants—Black and white—flocked to Detroit to take Ford up on his offer. They also sought work in the defense industries that resulted from U.S. engagement in the world wars. Detroit's economic system and access to jobs for migrants was not without flaws. Ford's hiring practices were discriminatory, and Black workers were often subjected to the dirtiest jobs. Defense industries also discriminated in their hiring, making it difficult for Black people to get the jobs that were part of their incentive for moving to the North.

The limits imposed on Black Detroiters in their work lives extended to their political lives. Although they were able to win election to state legislative positions, Black Detroiters' entrance into municipal politics occurred later than for their counterparts in New York and Chicago. Two facts distinguished the city and presented challenges for the Black population as it tried to gain political power. First, the city charter established a system of at-large elections that made it difficult for minority groups to organize themselves for political representation because, rather than campaign in their neighborhoods, they would have to seek votes across the entire city. Second, the absence of political parties meant that citizens did not have the option of organizing under a party banner. Eventually, in spite of these obstacles, Black people in Detroit were able to get elected to the city council.

In 1910, Detroit's Black population was slightly more than 1 percent—5,741—of the city's total. By the end of the first wave of the Great Migration in 1930, Black Detroiters constituted more than 7 percent of the total population. In 1940, Detroit's Black population was 149,119. Their numbers nearly doubled to 298,875 by 1950 and tripled to 482,405 by 1960, for a total increase of 333,104 (233 percent) over the span of twenty years. As a share of the electorate, Black people began the period accounting for almost 3 percent of the total voting age population (TVAP) in 1915. By 1970, because of normal population growth, continued in-migration, and white flight to suburban areas outside the city, the Black percentage of Detroit's TVAP was more than 43 percent. Table 3.1 shows this change in the city's population.

Like other northern cities, Detroit was segregated during the Great Migration period. Black citizens were confined to the Black Bottom and Paradise Valley neighborhoods. Black residents were in competition with immigrants and white southern migrants for space in the city. In the beginning, Black people lived in the East Side Colored District.[1] As the number of Black residents increased during the Great Migration, they began to push the boundaries of their confinements. Their pushing was intentional in some instances, as was the case with Dr. Ossian Sweet, who is discussed briefly below. Usually, however, they ended up in white neighborhoods because the Black areas were bursting at the seams.

This chapter proceeds in three parts. First, it describes the general political environment in Detroit, including information about the size of the Black population, the local party structure,

TABLE 3.1. DETROIT POPULATION, 1910–1970			
Year	Total population	Black population	Percentage Black
1910	465,766	5,741	1.23%
1920	993,675	40,838	4.11%
1930	1,568,662	120,066	7.65%
1940	1,623,452	149,119	9.19%
1950	1,849,568	298,875	16.16%
1960	1,670,144	482,405	28.88%
1970	1,511,482	660,428	43.69%

Source: U.S. Census Bureau (1910–1970), *Censuses of the Population, Statistics for Michigan, Detailed Characteristics of the Population.* Compiled by the author.

and the role of nongovernmental actors in shaping Detroit's nonpartisan politics. My essential claim is that the Great Migration influenced politics in the North in two ways: (1) by making Black voters a consideration of northern political parties and candidates and (2) by creating the potential for Black political office holding and the articulation of Black concerns in legislative bodies. Therefore, the second part of the chapter examines how mayoral candidates interacted with Black voters during the Great Migration period. Third, the chapter explains Black Detroiters' efforts to attain elected office themselves and considers the issues of interest to Black elected officials.

Political Environment

The political situation in Detroit differed from those of the other cities described in this book in two important ways, which had important consequences for how Black people experienced formal political participation there. During most of the period of interest, Detroit's municipal election system was at-large and nonpartisan. Whereas Black Americans in other cities were able to achieve descriptive representation in municipal politics relatively soon after the Great Migration began, Black Detroiters did not have representation on the city council until 1957. Other governmental bodies did have Black representation; for example,

Black candidates won election to the state legislature beginning in 1930. Others were elected to various positions in local government, such as ward constable and school board member.

The rules for elected office are an important determinant of access to political power. Since 1918, the Detroit city charter has called for nonpartisan elections and a council-mayor system of government.[2] Before that time, the city had forty-two partisan seats on the common council, with two individuals elected from twenty-one wards. In 1918, the Detroit Citizens League (DCL)—an organization of business leaders—worked to change the city charter to limit the number of elected officials on the city council and to eliminate political parties. The revised system replaced parties and wards with nine, nonpartisan city council members elected at-large from the entire city. The DCL described efficiency in government as its primary reason for wanting to change the city charter. However, people outside the business community understood the potential negative political impact of this change and challenged the DCL's motives. The organization's real goal, critics argued, was to limit the political influence of the growing population of southern migrants to the city. Under the DCL's new city charter, representation on the city council would effectively be limited to people in the business community. It would be very unlikely that communities of Black migrants, or white southerners, for that matter, would be able to elect representatives to the city council.

The Ford Influence on Politics

Henry Ford and the employees of the Ford Motor Company were very important to Detroit's economy and political environment. The Ford Motor Company was popular in the Black community for hiring Black workers when other companies refused to do so and for paying its Black employees the same wages as white employees in many instances. Southerners' desire to work for Ford was an important factor in much of the migration to Detroit. In addition to having an economic impact on the city, the corporation influenced city politics. Company leaders led a failed effort to reorganize the city government through their proposal of a 1914 city charter.

Ford himself worked with Black churches to support the Republican Party. He used monetary donations and job opportunities in his company to influence Black church leaders and parishioners (Dillard 2007: 102). He invested in Black churches in a number of ways, including some direct interactions with Black pastors that resulted in cash going to the church leaders (Bates 2012: 75). Ford was also deeply concerned about his employees' other political involvements. In particular, because he was opposed to having employees who were interested in union affiliation, Ford was curious about their potential interest in union organizations and activities (174). His position on unions extended to the Black workers he hired and was another reason for his surveillance of them.

Civil Society Institutions and Politics

In the absence of parties, other groups—including employers, labor unions, and civic organizations—organized politics. As mentioned above, the Ford Motor Company played an outsized role in city politics. Also important were two of the major labor unions, the Congress of Industrial Organizations (CIO) and the United Automobile Workers Union (UAW). Large civic organizations, including a host of citizen associations and homeowner groups, worked to organize the public for political purposes as well. The unions served some functions of political parties in nonpartisan spaces and worked closely with parties in parts of government where the party structure still operated (Rich 1989: 54). For example, the unions worked to educate and register Detroit citizens to vote, took positions on political issues, endorsed candidates, and worked on campaigns.

Black workers, who were often part of larger union organizations, also created their own union organizations. The Black organizations were clear at their inception about their concern for civil rights issues. For example, the National Alliance of Postal Employees[3] took up matters related to the work of the postal service, but its members were also focused on racial discrimination in their workplaces and surrounding areas (Miller 2016: 214). Black labor leaders in Detroit created the Trade Union Leadership Council (TULC) in 1957. The TULC was very active in local politics, encouraging Black candidates to run for office and eventually becoming an institution that political candidates looked to for endorsements that would help their standing among Black voters (Rich 1989: 76).

In the Black community, civic organizations took a slightly different shape. The leading organizations were political and social in nature; they were active in organizing and mobilizing people. These groups included the National Association for the Advancement of Colored People (NAACP) and the Urban League. Detroit was home to one of the oldest and largest chapters of the NAACP, which was active on race relations issues through protests and court cases. Such organizations as the Cotillion Club were started as social outlets but also engaged in political activities. As the Black population grew through the Great Migration, social organizations expanded their work to focus on education and voter registration of Black Detroiters (Thomas 1992: 254; Thompson 2001: 31). The club entertained visits from Black politicians and, in some instances, endorsed and supported them. For example, Charles Diggs Jr. visited them in 1950 when he was seeking support for his state senate race. The club was also influential in the election of William T. Patrick Jr. to the city council and "claimed credit for William Patrick's election to the common council in 1957" (Rich 1989: 57).

As in other cities, Black churches were central to political organizing during the Great Migration period. As Detroit's Black population grew, so did attendance at its Black churches. Politicians, church leaders, and parishioners understood the church as a central component in the process of bringing the community together. White politicians frequently interacted with Black pastors, hoping for their endorsements and for the opportunity to appear in front of their congregations. Black political aspirants also visited churches in the hope of securing Black support for their campaigns (Thomas 1992: 254). In 1965, the Reverend Nicholas Hood Sr. of the Plymouth Congregational Church—one of the city's most prominent pastors—won election to the Detroit City Council.

A number of white organizations also organized themselves for political purposes, with many of their efforts concentrated on working against racial progress for Black people in Detroit. Several of the white organizations were centered on neighborhoods. They sought to prevent neighborhood integration and to elect political leaders who would take anti-Black, anti-integration positions. One of the most powerful among these organizations was the DCL, which began as a government reform group. The group was very involved in local politics, working to make sure that the people elected to the city council were primarily concerned with real estate and business. The main example of this focus was the DCL's campaign to limit political involvement from newcomers to Detroit—including Black migrants—by changing the city charter in 1918.

Mayors and the Black Community

Detroit's electorate was highly fragmented regarding its opinions about the best structure for city government and approaches to the treatment of Black citizens. However, following the enactment of the 1918 charter, mayors with conservative racial ideologies successfully retained control of "the Northernmost Southern city" until the 1960s (Sugrue 2008: 132). The first mayor elected under the new city charter of 1918 was James J. Couzens, who came to politics after a long career as Ford's right-hand man. In his bid for mayor, he received the endorsement of the Ford Motor Company's management and two of the leaders in Detroit's Black community. However, Couzens had developed a reputation for discrimination against Black applicants while working as an executive at Ford, and the support from leaders in the Black and business communities did not translate into Black votes for Couzens. Black citizens remembered the employment opportunities lost as a result of Couzens's discrimination and chose not to support him in large numbers during his mayoral campaign. Despite the lack of support from the Black community, which was still a small portion—under 4 percent—of the city's total population, Couzens won the election (Bernard 2002; Chavis 1970).

The next election cycle, which included a local judicial election, shaped politicians' approach to coalition building with the Black community for many years. Although the 1920 judicial election was also nonpartisan, it was the first indication that Black Detroiters might assert their political independence from their bosses at the Ford Motor Company. The DCL slated a bloc of four judges to run for seats in the Recorder's Court for the 1920 campaign. Members of the court were supposed to be fair and independent, but the Recorder's Court judges usually voted together on court decisions. The result was that it had been nearly impossible for Detroit's Black community to achieve racial progress through the city courts. As they had in previous elections, members of management of the Ford Motor Company made it clear whom their employees should support: the DCL's slated candidates. However, Black voters had evidence that one of the four candidates allowed racist behavior in his court and was outwardly racist himself. Although the racist judge won the election, he placed eighth and ninth in Black wards. This result indicated to political observers that Black voters had actively sought to deny him one of the seven seats on the court (Bates 2012: 80).

In the same election cycle, Frank Murphy—another candidate for judge in the Recorder's Court, but without ties to the DCL—became one of the first white politicians in Detroit to actively solicit Black votes. Murphy believed that having judges run as a bloc was unfair and that the judges had been wrong in their handling of cases in the city. He listened to the concerns of many Black Detroiters, who did not believe they could receive fair trials in the city's court system. He campaigned on a promise that Black residents would receive fair treatment in his courts and won an overwhelming majority of votes in Black areas. Murphy's actions in the 1920 campaign created a template for campaigning to Black Detroiters that politicians used in future campaigns. Murphy was not successful in the 1920 election but would go on to win a seat on the Recorder's Court bench in 1923. Subsequent campaigns, including Murphy's own mayoral campaign in 1930, capitalized on the coalition that he built during his bid for the Recorder's Court (Fine 1973).

Couzens resigned as mayor in 1922 to accept an appointment to the U.S. Senate, leaving the position open to be filled through a special election in 1923. Frank Ellsworth Doremus won the 1923 special mayoral election but later resigned the office because of failing health. In the interim, John C. Lodge and Joseph A. Martin served as acting mayors, with Martin seeking to retain the position in the 1924 special election. Martin's opponents were Charles Bowles and John W. Smith. Martin was the candidate of the business lobby, who might have won the election except for the interference of Bowles. In the 1920s, the Ku Klux Klan (KKK) sought to gain control of politics through elected office. Bowles was the KKK's candidate and gained levels of support that were unexpected by Detroit's existing establishment politicians (Stoval 1983; see also Fox 2011).

On the other hand, Smith was a friend of Black Detroit. His campaign built on the coalition between Black and white ethnic voters that Murphy had assembled in 1920. Smith worked with Catholic and Jewish religious organizations to mobilize against the KKK candidate in white communities. In Black neighborhoods, he made campaign promises to Black voters that he would hire Black police officers (Bates 2012: 89). In the end, "Black Detroiters clearly influenced the outcome of the [1924] election" (Bates 2012: 89; Levine 1976: 137). Smith won the election and made good on his campaign promise to hire more Black police officers.

In the lead-up to the 1925 election for a full mayoral term, riots pushed Smith's support for Black issues to its limit. Violence erupted in Detroit as several Black families tried to move to neighborhoods beyond the "traditionally Black" areas of the Black Bottom and the East Side Colored District. In a reversal of his previous approach to interactions with the Black community, Smith cautioned Black leaders that they should work to maintain peace in the city. In this instance, that meant that they should stop fighting for open housing. Although he won the reelection campaign of 1925, this shift in his position would create problems for the following campaign (Bates 2012: 110).

The DCL and other groups in the city mounted a campaign against Smith in 1927, after disagreements over law enforcement and police hiring practices in the city. The DCL believed that a sitting member of the city council, John C. Lodge, who has previously served as interim mayor, was popular enough to unseat Smith in the coming election (Fragnoli 1982: 323). Working with leaders of a "citizens' committee" that included individuals from the business and labor communities of Detroit, Lodge declared his intention to run for mayor through a silent campaign. Lodge won the election of 1927 but lost the following mayoral election to Bowles, who had been the KKK-supported candidate for mayor in the previous two campaigns.

Race was an important issue during the 1929 campaign, as it had been during Bowles's previous campaigns for mayor. This time, he was running against Smith, the former mayor who was attempting to regain his position. Bowles maintained his support from the KKK and other white terrorist groups in the city by running as a "law and order" candidate (Fragnoli 1982). In the last days of the campaign, the Bowles team worked to stoke racial fear in white communities. For example, they disseminated an article from one of Detroit's Black news outlets in white neighborhoods, describing Black voters' support for Smith. Their goal was to suggest that Smith had previously been elected on the strength of Black votes; therefore, he would be supportive regarding Black issues. Bowles's campaign went on to advise the residents of white neighborhoods that it was imperative for them turn out in large numbers to prevent Smith's election.[4]

Bowles won the 1929 election but lost his seat as mayor in a recall election less than one year after taking the office. Citizens sought Bowles's dismissal over his business dealings with criminal elements. When it came time to fill Bowles's unfinished term, many in the Detroit community turned to Murphy. Murphy had endeared himself to the Black community through his

1920 campaign for the Recorder's Court, described above. Further, the Black community appreciated his work on the Ossian Sweet trial. Sweet, a migrant from Florida and a Black doctor in Detroit, had purchased a home in a white Detroit neighborhood. He and his family had been violently taunted by his white neighbors. In response, a shot rang out from the second floor of Sweet's home. The trial against Ossian Sweet resulted in a hung jury. Sweet's brother, Henry, was acquitted in a second trial related to the incident. Black Detroiters believed that the Sweet family had gotten a fair trial, in part because of Murphy's influence on the court.

Again in 1930, race became an important part of the mayoral campaign. Although he had just been removed from office, Bowles ran against Murphy in the election for the seat from which he had just been recalled. Murphy sought to win Black votes, while Bowles campaigned on the idea that he rejected Black support. Murphy actively sought the endorsement of leaders in the Black community and campaigned in Black churches and community meetings. Detroit's Black community rallied around Murphy and gave him an overwhelming share of its votes (Bates 2012: 126–130). Murphy won the special election to the mayor's office in 1930 by building on the coalition he had constructed during his 1920 campaign for judge, which included Black Detroiters, labor unions, and white European immigrant groups.

Black voters supported Murphy again when he ran for a full term in 1931. Murphy's opponent was Harold Emmons, who had support from Ford's political machine. As he had in other elections, Murphy campaigned heavily in Black areas of Detroit and won support from Black leaders in the city. Because Murphy's opponent had backing from Ford, Black leaders and voters had to be careful as they balanced their political preferences with their economic well-being. Many Black Ford employees feared that they might face retaliation for supporting Murphy, but they supported him anyway. In the end, Murphy won large shares of the Black vote in the primary and general elections. In keeping with his campaign commitments, Murphy worked to decrease levels of Black unemployment by establishing an "Unemployment Committee" in the office of the mayor during his tenure (Bates 2012).

In 1933, President Franklin Roosevelt appointed Murphy to the position of governor-general of the Philippines. Couzens was selected to serve the rest of Murphy's mayoral term. When the campaign for a full mayoral term approached, Couzens resigned his position as acting mayor to focus on the campaign. Couzens won the election for a full term as mayor of Detroit in 1934 and held the position until 1938.

Labor organizations had begun to think of Black voters as potential allies by the 1937 mayoral election. The UAW endorsed Patrick O'Brien, a liberal Democrat, for mayor. Labor forces sought to increase Black support for O'Brien by campaigning on issues that were important to them: law enforcement and police interactions, employment discrimination, and civil rights protections. However, O'Brien's support in Black circles was limited. His opponent in the race was Richard Reading, whom leading Black Detroiters considered a "friend of the negro" (Thomas 1992: 291). In spite of the increased outreach to Black communities by the union, Black voters opposed the labor candidate and supported Reading, who won the election.

During Reading's time in office, Detroit's problem of police brutality intensified. Leaders in the Black community created an organization called the Committee to End Police Brutality and attempted to convince Reading that he should hire a new police commissioner. The mayor chose to retain the sitting commissioner, which led to calls for his resignation by Black and white residents. During Reading's 1939 reelection bid, the mayor's inaction on the police issue became a major campaign issue and point of contention for Black voters in the city. Edward Jeffries, Reading's opponent for the mayor's seat, understood the gravity of this issue for Black voters and promised to fire the police commissioner if elected mayor (Meier and Rudwick 1979: 199). Reading's inaction cost him the support of the Black community, which was approaching 150,000 people by the time of the election. Jeffries won the election with support from large numbers of Black voters (Thomas 1992: 233).

Jeffries began his administration as the first Detroit mayor who was a New Dealer, prolabor, and racially liberal. He kept many of his campaign promises to Black voters, especially the promises made to increase the size of the Black workforce in city government. These actions helped Jeffries win his 1941 reelection bid with Black support. However, the positive relationship between Jeffries and the Black community did not last long because of problems with housing and policing.

Jeffries's politics became more conservative on racial issues over the course of his administration (Sugrue 1995). In a reversal of position, Jeffries openly stated his belief that public housing in Detroit should be segregated. After requests to end segregated housing in Detroit, Jeffries refused and clarified his position in a resolution: "The Detroit Housing Commission will in no way change the characteristics of any neighborhood in Detroit through occupancy standards of housing projects under their jurisdiction."[5] White Detroiters heavily favored his new stance, which would become an important part of his next mayoral campaign (Shaw 2009: 46; Sugrue 1995). Black voters began working with labor groups to form a liberal alliance. Their goal was to get Jeffries out of office in the 1943 mayoral campaign (Thomas 1992: 256).

Jeffries's opponent in 1943 was Frank Fitzgerald, who was supported by the UAW and the CIO. Fitzgerald promised Black voters that he would appoint a new police commissioner. The Black leadership in Detroit supported Fitzgerald's campaign, and Black areas of the city gave him overwhelming shares of their votes in the primary election. In the general election, Jeffries campaigned against Fitzgerald to white audiences on the idea that Black Detroiters had started a riot that had occurred in 1943. Further, he praised the police department's violent response to the instability as "magnificent" (Meier and Rudwick 1979: 204). Jeffries's campaign also argued that Fitzgerald must have gained popularity in the Black community by advocating for desegregated housing. The Jeffries campaign released materials in white neighborhoods that were designed to stoke fear, such as the following:

> FITZGERALD VICTORY MEANS STRATHMOOR AND COOLEY HIGH TO GET NEGRO FLOOD; IF FITZGERALD WINS, NEGROES WILL FLOOD AREA AND SOUTHWESTERN HIGH; MAYOR EXPOSES PLAN TO FORCE NEGROES INTO WHITE AREA. (Martin 1944: 10)

Fitzgerald responded to Jeffries, not by condemning his statements but by changing his previous positions to make his own racist appeals to white voters. This approach disappointed the Black community. Despite his posturing toward white voters late in the campaign, Fitzgerald got more support than Jeffries in Black neighborhoods; Black Detroiters thought of Fitzgerald as the lesser of two evils (Meier and Rudwick 1979). However, in the end, Jeffries beat Fitzgerald to retain the position of mayor because members of the white labor community divided their support. Instead of supporting the candidate who had been endorsed by the unions, many white Detroit voters responded to the racist appeals to fortify segregation in the city and cast their ballots for the incumbent.

In 1945, Jeffries's opponent was Richard Frankensteen, the vice president of the UAW and a supporter of open housing. The Jeffries camp brought race into the campaign via cards designed to worry white Detroiters about attempts to integrate their neighborhoods. Jeffries's campaign designed the materials to look as though they had been produced by the Frankensteen campaign. The cards included messages that would infuriate and mobilize voters in the white neighborhoods and downtown areas of the city. Two examples of the cards follow:

> Negroes Can Live Anywhere
> In Any Area—Any Section—of Detroit
> WITH FRANKENSTEEN MAYOR
> Negroes—Do Your Duty Nov. 6

> FORWARD NEGROES!
> Unite with Frankensteen for Mayor
> We Negroes Gave 21,572 Votes

> To Frankensteen in Primary
> LET'S PUT HIM IN NOV. 6
> A Negro Vote for Frankensteen is a
> Blow to White Exclusive Areas
> (Smith and Sarasohn 1946: 37)

The effect of the cards was to drive up the level of interest in the campaign and turnout for the election (Stovall 1983: 91–92). Jeffries won the 1945 election by 57,726 votes. However, Jeffries's racist tactics were not enough to sustain him in the following election. He lost the 1947 mayoral race to Eugene Van Antwerp, a conservative member of the city council, by a thin margin of just 18,767 votes.

The mayoral election of 1949 included a larger pool of candidates, who represented a broader array of positions on the ideological spectrum. Jeffries and Frankensteen, both of whom had been candidates in recent elections, declared that they would run for mayor again. Frankensteen and another candidate, George Edwards, were on Jeffries's political left. Edwards, who had also worked as a city administrator, was a very popular member of the city council, a war veteran, and an active participant in the labor union. Liberals in the city believed that Edwards would give them their first shot at the mayor's office since Murphy. Another candidate, Albert Cobo—a Republican real estate investor who was also the city treasurer—was the most conservative among those running for mayor in 1949.

As he had in previous elections, Jeffries used race as a wedge issue in the election. Cobo's campaign was explicitly focused on race and housing. He used race-baiting tactics to appeal to white voters but did so more aggressively and effectively than Jeffries. Both conservative campaigns cautioned white voters that liberals were too friendly with Black people. Both campaigns also continued the practice of trying to confuse voters in the city through political propaganda. Unlike during past election campaigns, Black voters were the target audience for false political messages during the 1949 contest. Both campaigns produced literature to persuade Black voters that the liberal candidates in the race did not actually espouse pro-Black positions. They hoped to confuse Black voters who, because the city was nonpartisan, might not have any other signals about the political positions of the candidates.

With the UAW organizing the election for Edwards, it seemed that conservatives would be defeated in 1949. However, liberal groups—Black people, white liberal sympathizers, labor leaders, and civic organizations—were unable to translate their work and coalition building into electoral victory. The aforementioned coalitions lacked support from a large, important group of Detroit voters: white union workers. They failed because rank-and-file white union members were willing to vote against their own economic interests for the sake of maintaining segregated neighborhoods. In the end, Cobo defeated Edwards in the 1949 campaign by winning in many of the white, working-class precincts (Sugrue 2008).

Once in office, Cobo enacted many policies that were hostile to Black Detroiters. He began an aggressive slum clearance and highway construction program with "improvement of central Detroit" as his stated goal. The effect was the construction of a highway through the Black community and the removal of longtime residents who lacked alternatives for housing (Sugrue 2014: 48). Cobo ended the Mayor's Committee on Race Relations, which had existed in various forms since the violence around the Sweet case. He also opposed fair employment practice laws designed to limit discrimination against Black workers. White voters continued to support his conservative approach to politics, and Cobo was reelected as mayor of Detroit two more times, in 1951 and 1953.

Louis Miriani became the mayor of Detroit in 1957 after Cobo died of a heart attack while still in office. Later that year, Miriani won election to office in his own right. He was even more conservative than Cobo on racial issues. Once in office, he dramatically increased police presence in Black neighborhoods through his anti-crime plan. "During the first forty-eight hours of the crackdown, Detroit police arrested more than six hundred people," many of the arrests without legitimate cause for suspicion (Turrini 1999: 12). Miriani began to change his stance on racial issues once it became clear that Black Detroiters were potentially important swing voters in local elections (Sugrue 2008). However, his initial positions and law enforcement practices in Black communities left a negative, indelible impression in the minds of Black voters. By the mayoral campaign of 1961, it was too late for Miriani to win over Black voters.

The Black population in Detroit had been growing rapidly over the decades of the Great Migration. By the 1960s, its numbers were formidable. Whereas Black Detroiters accounted for only 6 percent of the population at the beginning of the twentieth century, they accounted for one-third of the city population by the end of the 1960s. Black organizations, including the NAACP, the TULC, and the Detroit Cotillion Club, thrived in the growing community. These groups organized alongside the Black community at-large to increase the power of their voting bloc and to support a liberal mayoral candidate named Jerome Cavanagh.

In the lead-up to the 1961 mayoral contest, leaders in the Black community organized the 5+1 campaign to encourage Black Detroiters to vote strategically in the election. Although voters could cast nine votes for representatives to the city council, the campaign instructed Black voters to choose only five people for council seats plus cast one vote for Cavanagh as mayor (Rich 1989: 77). The goal was to ensure that five of the people who made it past the primary elections would be individuals sympathetic to Black issues. The campaign did not go as well as its architects hoped because limiting Black votes left space for conservatives to get nominated. However, it demonstrated that Black Detroiters had the capacity to unite themselves for strategic engagement in the city's governing systems. The result of the 5+1 effort was that Cavanagh and one white liberal, Mel Ravitz, advanced to the general election alongside a number of conservative candidates.[6]

The 1961 mayoral election was a referendum by the Black community on Miriani's heavy-handed use of law enforcement and a show of support for Cavanagh's liberal positions on civil rights issues. During his campaign, Cavanagh was clear about his intentions to support progress in civil rights. He won the mayoral election of 1961 by performing very well in Black neighborhoods and earning support from white voters (Thompson 2001: 31). Once elected, Cavanagh kept his campaign promises to Black voters by increasing the number of Black employees at City Hall and appointing a new police commissioner. But as a result of problems with police interactions in the city, the Black community's relationship with Cavanagh eventually deteriorated. In spite of these challenges, Cavanagh was reelected mayor in 1965. The 1961 election remains one of the most important in Detroit's history, as it was the Black community's first victory in determining who became the city's mayor.

Black Voters as the Balance of Power in Detroit Elections

I argue in this book that politicians' responsiveness to Black voters varies on the basis of (1) the interaction of the spatial distribution of Black people and the rules for election to office in the city and (2) the degree of party cohesion. Politicians in Detroit were not sensitive to segregation in the city or competition between factions in parties because neither was consequential to their ability to win elected office. With the changes brought by the 1918 city charter, white politicians eliminated parties as well as the possibility that individuals could be elected to municipal office as racial or ethnic representatives of their neighborhoods. For most of the mayoral elections, Detroit politicians were responsive to Black voters in ways that did not benefit them. White politicians in Detroit used race and civil rights as wedge issues to stoke fear in the white electorate and to mobilize white voters to support racially conservative candidates for political office.

Twenty-two mayoral elections occurred in Detroit following the new charter. I estimate the potential impact of the Black voting age population (BVAP) at three levels: 100, 67, and 50 percent. In Detroit, Black voters could have been the balance of power (BOP) in at least half of the mayoral elections during this

TABLE 3.2. BLACK VOTERS' BALANCE OF POWER POTENTIAL, DETROIT MAYORAL ELECTIONS, 1918–1965		
Black voting age population (BVAP) estimate		
100% of BVAP	67% of BVAP	50% of BVAP
19 of 22 elections	13 of 22 elections	11 of 22 elections

Source: U.S. Census Bureau (1910–1970), *Censuses of the Population, Statistics for Michigan, Detailed Characteristics of the Population.* Compiled by the author.

period. When comparing the margin of victory in mayoral elections to 100 percent of the BVAP, Black voters could have been the BOP in nineteen of the twenty-two elections, or 86 percent of the time. When I reduce the estimate of the Black voting age to 67 percent, Black voters could have been the BOP in thirteen of the twenty-two elections, or 59 percent of the time. Finally, Black voters could have been the BOP in eleven of the twenty-two elections—or half of the time—when I reduce the BVAP estimate to 50 percent. Although Black voters were the BOP in at least half of the mayoral elections from 1915 to 1965, Detroit's mayoral candidates did not respond positively to Black voters. Table 3.2 shows Black Detroiters' balance of power potential.

Another part of my argument is that that we should consider white politicians' beliefs about Black voters' political power and position as the BOP in elections to explain their behavior rather than focus on the actual votes of Black people. This is because politicians and political leaders frequently referenced Black voters' position as the BOP rather than their vote totals. Further, I assume that politicians and parties responded positively to Black voters when they viewed Black voters as the potential BOP in an election. I do not describe Black voters as the potential BOP in Detroit elections at the beginning of the period because the population was small. However, it is clear that the city's mayoral candidates did believe that Black voters had political power. Later in the period, we see evidence of the politicians' beliefs about the power of Black voters.

The evidence that liberal candidates believed that Black voters had power comes from their taking positions that spoke directly to Black voters' desires for their government. This behavior was true for Mayors Murphy, Jeffries (before 1943), Cavanagh, and a number of mayoral candidates who did not win elections. Murphy fulfilled a promise to reduce Black unemployment in the city. In his first campaign, Jeffries promised Black voters that he would support them by firing the police commissioner and hiring Black Detroiters to work in the city government. Cavanaugh made and, unlike Jeffries, kept his promise to fire the police commissioner. In each of these instances, candidates made a calculation that they needed Black voters to win their elections and modified their campaign approaches to win their support.

We know that conservative candidates believed that Black voters had political power because their campaigns expended resources to stifle Black participation and confuse Black voters. Take, for example, some of the conservative campaigns' uses of political propaganda. In the 1949 campaign, Jeffries and Cobo attempted to confuse and dissuade Black voters. If conservative candidates did not believe that Black voters would be consequential to the election, it should follow that they would not have cared whether or how Black voters were participating or supporting liberal candidates.

Also noteworthy is Detroit's conservative mayoral candidates' use of racial issues as a way to unify white voters. Examination of the campaigns from 1918 to 1965 indicates that politicians believed that white residents' fear of the growing Black population was salient enough to influence white voting behavior. This approach was true for most of the city's mayors, including Bowles, Jeffries (after 1943), and Cobo. Consider again the varying levels of racial propaganda in Detroit's mayoral elections during the Great Migration period. Candidates used white residents' panic about Detroit's growing Black population and potential integration of neighborhoods and schools to secure electoral support from white voters who seemed to have economic incentives to support liberal candidates.

Although politicians were responsive to Black Detroiters, and enough of them participated in the electorate to be the BOP, racially conservative mayors led Detroit for most of the period. The political situation in Detroit fits Chuck Stone's (1970) cri-

TABLE 3.3. DETROIT VOTING AGE POPULATION (VAP), BY PERCENTAGES, 1910–1970

Year	Total VAP	Black VAP	Percentage Black VAP
1910	150,017	4,330	2.89%
1920	360,040	30,579	8.49%
1930	991,100	81,968	8.27%
1940	1,088,739	99,212	9.11%
1950	1,267,565	204,680	16.15%
1960	1,065,987	268,956	25.23%
1970	940,632	359,006	38.17%

Source: U.S. Census Bureau (1910–1970), *Censuses of the Population, Statistics for Michigan, Detailed Characteristics of the Population.* Compiled by the author.

tique of the BOP theory—in short, that Black voters are unable to change the outcome of elections when the white vote is unified against them. To make sense of this argument, let's consider the entire population of the city. Although the population included enough Black people to account for the BOP in many of the city's elections, the total electorate included even more white people. As Table 3.3 shows, Black voters comprised less than 25 percent of the TVAP for most of the period. It was not until Black Detroiters constituted a significant percentage of the Black population in the city that they could help determine electoral outcomes. Further, even when their share of the electorate increased, in the 1960s, they needed to work in coalition with like-minded groups to have a major influence on municipal elections. For example, in the 1961 election of Cavanaugh, Black Detroiters worked with unions and white liberal organizations to influence the election. Coalitions would also be necessary to facilitate the election of the first Black representative to the city council, which I describe in the next section.

Black Political Office Holders in Detroit

While Black Detroiters fought to influence politics through civil organizations and labor unions, they also struggled to win elected office in the city. I argue in this book that the Great Migration was an important determinant in the likelihood that Black people would be elected to office. Although the Black population of Detroit grew throughout the Great Migration, Black people in the city faced structural barriers to attainment of elected office that slowed Black election to legislative bodies. Chief among the obstacles were changes in the state's party system and method for choosing individuals for public office. These problems were especially pronounced in local government elections. The aforementioned city charter change that occurred not long after the start of the Great Migration prevented Black representation in the city council for many years. In the state legislature, plans for slum clearance made it difficult to maintain cohesive Black neighborhoods and, by extension, Black electorates. Yet in spite of the challenges, twenty-eight Black people were able to represent Detroit in the city's common council, state legislature, and congressional districts between 1915 and 1965. Twenty of the twenty-eight—71 percent—were migrants.[7]

The following section describes Black elected officials' political involvement in Michigan's legislative bodies. I begin with a discussion of the state legislature, where Black people were first elected. Next, I discuss Black involvement in the city's legislative body, the common council. Finally, I consider Detroit's representatives to the U.S. Congress. For each of these legislative bodies, I also briefly consider Black representatives' policy priorities to show how they brought attention to issues of concern for Black communities. As part of the analysis, I highlight elected officials who were migrants as well as those who were concerned about issues of particular interest to Black migrant populations.

Black Detroiters in the State Legislature

Black people first participated in Detroit politics in the late 1800s. William W. Ferguson—a Detroit native—served in the state legislature from 1893 to 1896. James W. Ames—a migrant from New Orleans, Louisiana—was elected in 1901. At that time, Black elected representatives participated in politics as Republicans, and they earned their positions as rewards for their work with the Republican Party. However, rule changes would make Ames the last Black person to come into the state legislature through a meritorious party nomination. It became much more difficult for Black people to hold political office in the state legislature following the rule change. As a result, no Black people served in the Michigan state legislature until almost thirty years later, when the Great Migration was in full swing and Charles Roxborough was elected (Orr 1993).[8] By comparison, Black people had been serving in the Illinois and New York legislatures since 1915 and 1917, respectively.

By 1930, enough Black Detroiters lived in the third senatorial district to send a representative to the state legislature. Roxborough, a migrant from Louisiana, won election to the state legislature and served one term. Charles Diggs Sr., who was elected in 1936, followed him in the position and remained in the office for many years. The Michigan state legislature had continuous Black representation from Diggs Sr.'s election onward. That Black politicians in Michigan had more success attaining positions in the state legislature and in the U.S. Congress, where the districts are narrowly defined, highlights the challenge of running in a nonpartisan, citywide election. For example, Diggs Jr., who successfully won election to the Michigan state senate in 1951, lost his campaign for a seat on the city council in 1953. In 1955, Diggs Jr. ran for Congress and won that election.

Black women in Detroit had more success getting elected to political offices than women in New York or Chicago. Charline White—a migrant from Atlanta, Georgia—won election to the Michigan House of Representatives in 1950. After two unsuccessful bids for the state senate in 1950 and 1951, Cora Brown—presented in this book's Introduction—became the first Black woman elected to any state senate in 1952. Together, Brown and White—pictured in Figure 3.1—served as the only female state legislators following the 1952 election. In the following decade, three additional women served in the state legislature: Maxcine Young, Daisy Elliott, and Rosetta Ferguson were all elected to the Michigan House of Representatives in the 1960s.

Figure 3.1. Migrant women taking charge: State Senator Cora M. Brown and State Representative Charline R. White, January 1953. (Associated Press.)

In addition to the demographic changes brought by the Great Migration, the electoral situation in the Michigan state legislature was also heavily influenced by the 1962 Supreme Court case *Baker v. Carr.* The court ruled that political boundaries should be drawn with respect to the number of people living in a jurisdiction rather than arbitrary boundaries. Following the ruling, Michigan's congressional and legislative lines were called into question and eventually changed through a series of court cases. After the lines were redrawn, the number of Black people in the state legislature from Detroit doubled over what it had been in the previous decades. The changing nature of partisanship in the state capital was another significant development of the 1960s. In the 1964 election, control of the state legislature changed from the Republican Party to the Democratic Party.

Legislative Concerns of Black Detroiters in the State Legislature

During the Great Migration era, Black legislators in Michigan had concerns similar to those of their counterparts in New York and Illinois. Anti-discrimination legislation, with a focus on jobs and housing, was their top priority. These issues had specific impacts on migrants, who expected that they would be able to find work and housing when they left the South. Fair employment laws would guarantee that migrants could actually find jobs and get hired in industry once they arrived in the North. Black State Senators Diggs Jr. and Brown, along with Edwards in the state house of representatives, fought for the establishment of a Fair Employment Practices Committee (FEPC) in the state of Michigan and worked on legislation to outline its abilities.[9] Although they were successful in getting the bill through the legislature in 1955, they were disappointed that legislative bargaining eventually eliminated the committee's ability to subpoena individuals accused of discrimination.[10]

Housing in Detroit was scarce and expensive during the Great Migration period. As Black people flooded into the city during the migration, landlords rented units that were barely inhabitable in some instances. Black elected officials worked to ensure access to housing for the city's Black residents. As part of a larger civil rights bill, State Senator Basil Brown and Representative George H. Edwards sought to outlaw discrimination in all housing constituting three or more units—whether public or private.[11] James Del Rio, who was a successful Realtor and real estate investor before his election to the state house of representatives, also did noteworthy work on housing. State Senator Coleman Young fought to ensure that the city provided housing accommodations for residents before it launched a slum clearance program during his time in the state legislature.[12] Young would later become the city's first Black mayor.[13]

Black people in Detroit faced serious problems with policing and law enforcement throughout most of the period of interest. As discussed earlier in the chapter, policing in the city became a campaign issue for mayoral candidates as they sought to manage racial politics. Issues of policing were also important to Black members of the state legislature. In 1957, Frederick Yates and Charline White sponsored a resolution in the state house of representatives to request that the Detroit Common Council investigate conditions in the city jail. The state representatives were concerned about "alleged inhuman and vicious practices" in the city's prison work program, which was funded by the state.[14] In another example, a police shooting drew attention from Black state legislators and the lone Black city councilman. After police shot and killed Cynthia Scott for resisting arrest in July 1963, Black state legislators and civic organizations from Detroit requested an in-depth investigation of her death.[15]

Black legislators did not limit themselves to issues that were explicitly concerned with race; some were concerned about a variety of policy issues. Many of the bills sponsored by Basil Brown, the majority floor leader in the state senate, dealt with financial regulations and taxation.[16] Maxcine Young worked on a bill for gender pay equity that passed in the state house of representatives.[17] Representative Horace White, concerned that the public was losing confidence in elected officials, introduced legislation that would require lobbyists to register in the state and limit their gifts as a way to prevent bribery.[18]

Detroit's Black legislators were not a monolith. They disagreed on some things, including their approaches to getting legislation passed, what should be a legislative priority, and who should be elected to office. In one instance, members of the state legislature took different positions on a measure about the placement of photographs on state identification cards. Representative Maxcine Young—who was the chair of the Traffic and Safety Committee in the legislature—was working to determine the status of the state's drivers' licenses. She was part of a group of legislators who wanted to add photos to the state documents. Young's Black counterparts—including David S. Holmes Jr. and Rosetta Ferguson—argued that adding photos to the state IDs would create potential for discrimination against minorities, calling the bill a "backward step in the struggle for Negro equality."[19] Young argued that the bill was not discriminatory and encouraged members of the house to support the legislation. "I just don't see it at all," Young said. "This is a bad amendment to a good bill." In the end, members of the legislature supported Young's push for the bill, and it passed with the requirement for photos intact.

Legislative Concerns Related to Black Migrants in the State Legislature

Another goal of this book is determining whether participants in the Great Migration differed in their political/legislative activity from Black legislators who were born in the North. I suggest that migrant legislators might have been especially interested in political issues of concern to other migrants. For example, I expect that some legislation might have named migrants and specifically focused on their challenges. Further, I expect that elected officials who were migrants would have been concerned with other migrants' ability to get work and find adequate housing. My findings are consistent with these expectations. Although there was not an overwhelming focus on issues that were specific to migrants as distinct from the universe of Black people living in Detroit, some pieces of legislation were specific to migrants. These included requests to study issues of concern to migrants and legislation to provide protections for agricultural migrant workers. For example, in 1960, Frederick Yates, a migrant from Arkansas, proposed a commission to study issues of specific interest to migrants, including housing and education.[20]

In addition to Black Americans, a number of other groups migrated to Michigan during the Great Migration. Larger in numbers, although not in percentages, was a group of white southerners. Mexican immigrants also composed a significant portion of the migrant population, especially in the later years of the period. At varying levels, all three groups of people worked in Michigan's agricultural economy. They came directly to Detroit from the South or went out into the state's rural areas from Detroit during the harvest season from April through October.[21] Migrant agricultural workers—one-third of whom were women and children—faced harsh living conditions and low pay during the harvest season. Black Michigan legislators, recalling their own struggles as migrants, worked to secure legislation that would provide protections for them. State Representative Edgar Currie worked to pass legislation to protect migrant agricultural workers.[22] In each of the ten years that he served in the state legislature, Currie introduced legislation to protect migrants. In a few instances, he was successful in getting the legislation through the state house of representatives. However, because of strong opposition from the farm lobby in the state, the bills often died in the state senate.[23]

In 1963, David Holmes and James Bradley—migrants from Covington, Kentucky, and Hope, Arkansas, respectively—worked to reintroduce and pass Currie's legislation to protect migrant farm workers. In describing the legislation, Holmes recounted the work of a migrant from Florida who toiled for an entire summer, only to earn a paltry $1.25. He also described his own experience as an agricultural migrant for one summer when he traveled from South Carolina to Rhode Island, trying to earn money for college. The 1963 legislation would have regulated the behavior of the individuals who recruited migrant workers, known as "crew leaders," so they did not commit wage theft. The bill would have also provided health, housing, and sanitation benefits to the migratory workers commensurate with what existed for other individuals in that community.[24] Black legislators were not successful in securing the legislation to protect migrants. By 1965, the state's liberal governor was hopeful that party change in the legislature might lead to legislation at some point in the near future.[25]

Black Detroiters in Local Elected Positions

Black Detroiters' electoral situation was more precarious on the city council than in the state legislature. Beginning in 1882, Dr. Stanley C. Watson—a migrant from South Carolina—served two terms on the city council (Stovall 1983: 23). Not long after his term in office, the method of getting into public office changed. When Watson served on the city council, individuals on the council and in the state legislature received their positions at party conventions as rewards for their work rather than through engagement with the electorate. By 1901, however, the system changed to require individuals to win the primary election vote of their parties and compete in a general election to hold office. It was tremendously difficult for Black people to be elected to the city council or the state legislature following this change.

Another structural hurdle to Black representation on the city's common council came from the 1918 change to Detroit's city charter, which I describe at a number of points in this chapter (see also Bates 2012: 34; Orr 1993: 109). The 1918 revision, which coincided with the growth of the Black population, made it more difficult for individuals to get elected as representatives of their racially homogenous communities.[26] Whereas the old system called for the election of forty-two members to the Detroit City Council from residence-based districts through a party system, the new charter called for nine nonpartisan city council members to serve the city at-large, without regard to neighborhoods. Proponents of the change argued that it would make the city government more efficient: rather than having to work through the concerns of two members from each residential district, the council could focus its attention on the concerns of a smaller, potentially better equipped, and highly educated group of politicians. The outcome was the exclusion of the Black population from municipal elected office, in spite of its tremendous growth during the Great Migration (Katzman 1973; Stovall 1983). Following the change, thirty-nine years would pass before the election of a Black city council member.

Yet Black Detroiters were not deterred from seeking a seat on the city council by the structural barriers inherent in the city charter. A number of them ran for office before they actually won representation.[27] Of note is the city council campaign of Rev. Charles Hill, who ran in 1945 and 1949. In the 1945 election, Hill made it past the primary stage.[28] In the 1945 election, Hill placed ninth out of sixty-six candidates, the highest ranking of any Black person who had run for the position previously.[29] Yet Hill was not elected to the city council, in spite of this strong showing in the 1945 primary, because of strong counter-efforts by Edward Jeffries's mayoral campaign (Dillard 2007: 162–164).[30] Hill ran for the position again in 1949. That time, he qualified for the general election but failed to make it into the top nine as was required to earn a seat on the city council.[31]

By the mid-1950s, people in the Black community had a sense that the conditions were finally right for a Black person to be elected to the council. In the 1957 election, a few Black candidates ran for a seat on the city council and three—including two migrants and one Detroit native—made it past the primary election. Edwards (from Macon, Georgia) moved forward to the general election along with Diggs Jr. (from Detroit).[32] And after a number of unsuccessful attempts, the third of the Black candidates in 1957, William T. Patrick Jr., won representation for Black Detroiters on the city council in that election.

Patrick was a migrant who had been born in Washington, D.C., and had graduated from Howard University. His candidacy and campaign had been carefully designed to speak to Black issues while demonstrating to white voters that he was a safe bet. Supported by the TULC, which was an organization created by thirteen Black labor activists, he earned 52,859 votes in the primary election, coming in ninth out of eighteen on the primary election ballot.[33] In the general election, with 141,878 votes, he came in eighth out of nine candidates.[34] The victory made Patrick the first Black person ever elected to the Detroit City Council.[35] In interviews following the election, he asserted that he was a representative of all people—not just Black Detroiters.[36] Patrick told the *Detroit Free Press*, "I have nothing in mind for Negroes alone. That is not the spirit in which I was elected, and I will not have it any other way."

However, Patrick became increasingly interested in problems that affected Black Detroiters while on the council. By 1963, after having observed events unfold during his tenure, Patrick's tone had changed. He told the local newspaper that housing was "THE pivotal race problem, and failure to provide it is the cause of continuing tensions."[37] In response, he worked on anti-discrimination measures in housing.[38] The legislation—which did not earn the votes to pass on the city council—would have prevented discrimination in the sale and rental of housing in Detroit.[39]

Patrick also worked on issues with policing in the city. He worked to integrate Detroit's police force by hiring more Black officers. He was also concerned with the treatment of Black Detroiters by the police. As mentioned earlier in this chapter, Patrick was among a group of Black Detroiters working to initiate an investigation into the shooting death of twenty-four-year-old Cynthia Scott, a Black woman who was killed while she was allegedly resisting arrest. Always careful to balance his service to Black people with his service to the broader Detroit community, Patrick requested that the police also investigate the shooting of Kenneth Evans, a young white male who had been murdered by police around the same time as Scott.[40]

By all accounts, Patrick was a highly effective and well-respected member of the city council. His fellow councilmen nominated him to serve as the chair of the Wayne County Board of Supervisors.[41] He also served as the common council president. In December 1963, Patrick resigned his position to become a corporation lawyer at Michigan Bell Telephone Company. In the next municipal election, Black Detroiters elected Nicholas Hood Sr. to the Detroit City Council.[42] Black people have continually served on the city council ever since.

The U.S. Congress

Although Chicago elected a Black member of Congress in 1929 and New York sent one in 1945, Detroit would not elect a Black congressional representative until 1955. Black Detroiters were aware of their political potential. For example, they once mounted a campaign to elect three Black people to the U.S. Congress. In 1962, the *Illustrated News*—a controversial Black news pamphlet—argued that it might be possible to elect a representative from the First, Thirteenth, and Fifteenth Congressional Districts. Albert B. Cleage's pamphlets argued that the Black community should work together to elect what he dubbed "the Freedom Slate": Frederick Yates for the Fifteenth Congressional District, Russell S. Brown for the First Congressional District, and Charles Diggs Jr. for the Thirteenth Congressional District. Cleage also advocated for the election of Joe B. Sullivan for prosecutor. In the end, only Diggs was successful in his bid.

Once Black Detroiters did begin to get elected to Congress, they were able to win multiple seats in the House of Representatives sooner than Black residents from the other Great Migration cities. Diggs Jr., a Detroit native who had been active in politics through the state legislature, was the first to represent Detroit in Washington and held his seat in Congress until 1980. In 1964, John Conyers, also a Detroit native, became the second Black person elected to represent Detroit. Conyers's election to represent the Fourteenth Congressional District made Michigan the first state with two Black people serving concurrently in Congress.

Conclusion

The political experiences of Black people in Detroit were powerfully shaped by the timing of their migration to the city and the structure of the city government. Although large numbers of Black migrants were settling in the city to look for work in the automobile and war industries, the Black population did not reach a critical mass for local politics until the 1960s. However, their presence did influence mayoral campaigns. As the Black population grew, so did the use of race as a wedge issue in the mayoral elections. Detroit's conservative mayoral candidates sought to elicit fear in white citizens about the integration of their neighborhoods. Candidates often persuaded union members to reject their organizations' endorsements in favor of anti-Black political positions. Conservative candidates won elections to the mayor's seat for most of the Great Migration period, except for Frank Murphy's 1930 and 1931 elections and until the 1961 election of Jerome Cavanaugh.

Detroit's revised city charter, which specified nonpartisan, at-large elections, was among the greatest impediments to political progress for Black people at the municipal level. In Detroit, Black voters' potential position as the BOP was stifled by the 1918 decision to create a system that would be resistant to the demands of minority groups. Without political parties, Detroit lacked some of the nuance and diversity in its local political debates that occurred in New York and Chicago. Often, race was the central issue in the city's mayoral campaigns. The vast majority of the white population organized in opposition to candidates who seemed sensitive to Black interests.

Beyond the challenges in mayoral politics, Detroit's nonpartisan, at-large system also delayed the election of Black residents to the city council. No Black person held a position in the city's legislative body until the 1957 election of William T. Patrick. Fortunately, another Black Detroiter—Nicholas Hood Sr.—was able to win election to the city council after Patrick's departure. However, demonstrating the sustained challenge of winning at-large elections, not more than one Black person at a time would serve on the council during the period.

Although Black people faced challenges getting elected to city positions, they were able to win election to the state legislative and congressional seats. Black people began to represent

Detroit in the state legislature beginning in 1930 and continued to get elected from then on. As legislators, Black Detroiters were concerned with a variety of issues related to Black life at the time, including discrimination in housing and labor. As the number of Black people living in the state increased, so did the number of Black people who were elected to the state legislature. Changes in Michigan's reapportionment process following *Baker v. Carr* were also an important factor contributing to the increase in the number of Black elected officials in the state legislature.

Black officials in Detroit brought concerns to the political agenda that might not have received attention absent their election to office. As members of the Black community who lived with these specific problems, Black elected officials brought a perspective that helped make the state's political agenda responsive to Black voters. For example, in at least one instance, state legislators who were also migrants worked on issues of specific concern to migrant communities. The proposed laws did not always pass in their respective legislative bodies, but their consideration was also important to the development of civil rights during the period. Without the influx of Black residents resulting from the Great Migration, the number of Black people in elected office doubtless would have been fewer. Further, there is a great likelihood that their issues might not have been considered as often without members of the race introducing them in various legislative settings.

4

New York

New York City has been home to more Black people than any other city outside the South since the Great Migration began. New York has also been home to some of the most recognizable participants in the Great Migration. Although we do not often think about them in these terms, many of the artists, musicians, and activists of the Harlem Renaissance were migrants: Zora Neale Hurston and Augusta Savage were from Florida, Louis Armstrong and Bessie Smith were from Louisiana and Tennessee, and Walter F. White was from Atlanta, Georgia.[1] Likewise, participants in the Great Migration were also important to the story of politics in New York City. They were among the most influential people working to organize the Black community for political participation. A. Philip Randolph, originally from Florida, moved to New York to pursue a career as an actor and later became an important figure in the civil rights movement. Upon arriving in New York City from North Carolina, Edward Austin Johnson—discussed in the book's Introduction—observed the lack of Black representation in local government and fought to change it. Over the fifty years under consideration in this book, Johnson and others like him would push the political apparatus to recognize Black residents of the city.

TABLE 4.1. NEW YORK CITY POPULATION, 1910–1970			
Year	Total population	Black population	Percentage Black
1910	4,766,883	91,709	1.92%
1920	5,620,048	152,467	2.71%
1930	6,930,446	327,706	4.73%
1940	7,454,995	458,444	6.15%
1950	7,887,380	749,080	9.50%
1960	7,781,984	1,087,931	13.98%
1970	7,894,862	1,668,115	21.13%

Source: U.S. Census Bureau (1910–1970), *Censuses of the Population, Statistics for New York, Detailed Characteristics of the Population.* Compiled by the author.

At the beginning of the Great Migration, Black voters accounted for 1.9 percent of the population, a number that had grown to 21.1 percent by 1970.[2] In 1910, New York's Black population was 91,709, accounting for less than 2 percent of the city's residents. In the next decade, the number would grow to 152,467, and it doubled to 327,706 in the 1930 Census. The number of Black residents continued to grow steadily after World War II and increased again to 458,444 in 1940 and 749,080 in 1950. By the end of the period, 1,087,931 Black people were living in New York City, comprising almost 14 percent of the total population. Table 4.1 shows the change in New York City's population from 1910 to 1970.

Black New Yorkers lived in various parts of the city between 1915 and 1965. They were scattered across Brooklyn, the Bronx, and Queens in small numbers. At the beginning of the period, the largest number of them lived in various parts of Manhattan. Before settling in Harlem, they moved northward through the borough from Greenwich Village, to the Tenderloin, to the San Juan/Lincoln Square neighborhoods (Osofsky 1971). Two factors delayed Black residents' entrance into electoral politics: the sheer size of New York City following the 1898 consolidation and Black New Yorkers' settlement across the boroughs rather than in a single, contained area (Biondi 2003: 208). Plans by mainstream party organizations to "crack" predominantly Black districts further thwarted their attempts to get elected to public office, even after their numbers had grown in the city.[3] By 1917, Harlem was the first area with a Black population large enough to command political representation in the state assembly. By the 1940s, the Black populations of Brooklyn and the Bronx were also substantial enough to drive the election of Black political representatives from those areas (Lewinson 1974; see also Osofsky 1971).

The immigration of Black people from other nations is another important part of the story of the Great Migration in New York. Whereas the word *immigrant* was synonymous with white Southern and Eastern Europeans in Chicago and Detroit, a number of immigrants in New York City came from the West Indies. Like Black southern migrants, Black West Indians began immigrating to New York in the early twentieth century, seeking opportunities to work (Greer 2013; see also Rogers 2006). Once in the United States, West Indian migrants fully participated in American life alongside southern Black migrants. They often lived in the same neighborhoods and worked through the same political organizations. Although they are not considered migrants under the definitions in this book, their role in shaping Black New Yorkers' politics is noteworthy.[4]

This chapter begins with a discussion of New York's political environment, including its complicated party system. Then, I examine Black political interactions with the city's mayoral candidates and associated party factions. The attention to mayoral candidates includes a discussion of New York's Black voters as the potential balance of power (BOP) in elections. Finally, I consider the political activity of the Black elected officials who held positions in the board of aldermen, the city council, the state legislature, and the U.S. House of Representatives. I highlight the political contributions of Black migrants among the general interests of all Black elected officials during the period.

Political Environment

Understanding the role of Black people in New York politics during the Great Migration requires attention to several moving parts: the two major political parties, anti-Tammany reform movements, and third parties. The party system in New York has always been complex, with the two major political parties being active alongside smaller party organizations within both parties as well as various third parties. Within the general structure of the Democratic and Republican Parties were numerous political clubs, usually based in smaller neighborhood subdivisions of the boroughs. For Black New Yorkers, segregation in the major parties also led to Black political clubs that existed outside the "regular" party structure.

Like Black people in most of the nation, Black New Yorkers typically identified as Republicans in their early political interactions. Some of the Black affinity for the Republican Party in New York State went back to the party's support for Black suffrage in the late 1800s. At the 1867 New York State Constitutional Convention, many members of the Democratic Party either rejected the idea of Black suffrage outright or suggested that the question of suffrage be put before the white electorate of the state. By contrast, most Republicans in the state supported equal access to the ballot box for Black New Yorkers. When it became clear that the question of Black suffrage might derail the possibility of a revised state constitution, Democrats and Republicans agreed to consider the issues as separate ballot questions. Once New York Republicans gained control of the state legislature, they found a work-around for providing Black suffrage by voting to ratify the Fifteenth Amendment to the U.S. Constitution. But in spite of the Republican Party's attempts to provide unfettered access to the ballot box, the measure failed due to lack of support (Scheiner 1965: 171). Black New Yorkers would not get the ability to vote until the Fifteenth Amendment passed in 1870.

Another reason Black New Yorkers were more supportive of the Republican Party was because it was more willing to support Black attempts to hold elected and appointed offices. Once Black people were able to freely participate in elections, they faced discrimination in their attempts to win nominations for political offices. Whereas the early Democrats of Tammany Hall routinely sought to exclude Black New Yorkers from politics by relegating them to segregated clubs and requiring that they subordinate themselves to white party officials, the Republican Party was more willing to nominate them for political offices.

The Democratic Party of New York was noteworthy for Tammany Hall, its strong political machine that controlled many aspects of politics in the city. Tammany was especially powerful in New York politics at the beginning of the Great Migration period, controlling who was nominated for political offices and who benefited from patronage in the city. In addition, Tammany influenced the structure of the city's governing bodies, which changed several times between 1915 and 1965. Party leadership was organized according to state assembly district boundaries. These state legislative assembly districts were further divided into election districts. Within the election districts were captains—that is, party members most closely connected to constituents (Walter and Jones 1989: 58). Before 1938, assembly district leaders were elected by party leaders, which meant that Tammany could keep tight control of who had power in neighborhoods.[5] The process changed in 1938, making assembly district leaders for a local area elected through popular vote. The new system also called for each district to have male and female co-leaders.

In 1898, Tammany Hall established a Black club, the United Colored Democracy (UCD).[6] The stated goal of the UCD was to organize the Black community to provide votes for Tammany. However, the UCD's citywide nature decreased the political influence of the Black community because political power in New York was vested in the assembly districts rather than in the city as a whole. Accordingly, a community's ability to control its assembly districts meant it would also control political nominations, patronage, and other political benefits. Black Democrats were at a disadvantage in their assembly districts because they were required to work through the UCD instead of organizing themselves in their assembly districts as their non-Black counterparts did. Tammany effectively diluted Black Democrats' local power by requiring them to share decision-making authority with Democrats across the city rather than by limiting the decisions to smaller, predominantly Black groups in neighborhoods. In other words, even when the Black population represented a majority of the electorate in an assembly district, its political decisions were subject to approval from white leaders in other parts of the city (Katznelson 1973: 70). Also problematic was that members of the UCD got few benefits for their success in turning out Black voters. They often had to fight to be nominated for elected positions or appointments to civil service positions.

In addition to the segregated clubs created by the parties, Black New Yorkers created their own political clubs.[7] These clubs varied in their political ideologies, aims, and goals. In some instances, individuals were seeking to assert their independence from machine leaders or Black leaders of the submachines. In other instances, Black New Yorkers formed their own clubs because white party organizations refused to nominate them for political office. What the clubs had in common was a desire to see their members and allies elected to office and to see their political concerns manifest as policy. For example, a Black Republican club strategized for Edward Austin Johnson to win a seat in the state assembly in 1917.

Black New Yorkers began their political participation as Republicans but moved into the Democratic Party in the early part of the Great Migration period. One of the initial examples of Black support for Democrats occurred when John Smith—a Black Tammany Democrat—was elected alderman with the support of Black voters in 1921. Whenever Democrats were out of power or faced a threat from reform factions, they turned to Black New Yorkers for electoral support (Walter and Jones 1989). Thus, the first major movements of Black New Yorkers into the Democratic Party occurred while Tammany was out of power during the Fiorello La Guardia era of the 1930s. The transition into the Democratic Party was rocky because many Black people believed that it was foolish to align with Democrats. Further, Tammany was viewed as unhelpful to Black causes because its members participated in and/or remained silent about issues of police brutality in the city (Lewinson 1974: 45). Nonetheless, by the 1940s, most Black people and Black political clubs had consolidated into the mainstream Democratic Party.

Third Parties

Third-party candidates were viable in New York City elections in ways they were not in Detroit or Chicago for at least two reasons. First, New York's fusion party system allowed individuals to run on more than one party line. Second, the major party organizations were very divided, which affected the ways that voters and candidates interacted. When the Democratic and Republican Parties failed to take positions that were beneficial to Black voters in the early twentieth century, many of them turned to third-party organizations as a way to engage in politics. In particular, they were active in the Communist, Socialist, Progressive, and American Labor Parties. These parties grew in their popularity among Black voters because they proved more willing to engage with issues related to ending segregation and redistributing wealth for poor Americans. Although these parties struggled internally as they sought to build relationships in the Black community, they proved themselves more receptive to Black political involvement than the two major parties (Ali 2008; Biondi 2003).

Migrants' willingness to run as third-party candidates helped motivate the Democratic Party machine to respond to pleas for Black representation (Ali 2008). Third parties recognized Black voters' potential to help them win elections and were among the first political organizations to nominate them for elected office. In a number of instances, Black third-party candidates' vote shares were notable. For example, in 1947, Ada B. Jackson—a migrant from Georgia—ran for a citywide seat on the Brooklyn City Council and garnered 23 percent of the vote in her election (Biondi 2003: 51). She lost to the Republican candidate for the office, but the Democratic Party noticed her ability to get votes. As a result of her campaign, Democrats slated a Black candidate for that state assembly seat in the next election. Later, in a 1949 campaign for Manhattan borough president, the American

Labor Party nominated Ewart Guinier. He earned one hundred thousand votes, or 38 percent of the total (211–212).

Civic and Religious Organizations

Unlike Detroit, where there were few formal ways to engage in politics for Black people, New York had many avenues for participation. The city's Black churches and civic organizations were important, but they were not as central a part of New York's Black political community. Politicians and parties engaged these groups only when necessary to demonstrate political will. For example, there were calls for community organizations to support Alderman Charles H. Roberts—a migrant from South Carolina—as he lobbied the city to open a bathhouse in Harlem.[8] A notable exception was the political activity of the congregation of the Abyssinian Baptist Church, which helped Adam Clayton Powell Jr. become the first Black person to be elected to the U.S. Congress from New York. Although civic and religious organizations were active in New York's Black political communities, they often took more of a backseat than they did in Detroit or Chicago.

Mayoral Politics

New York City's mayoral candidates were responsive to Black voters in ways that were mostly positive from 1915 to 1965. Unlike Detroit and Chicago, where some mayoral candidates took positions in direct opposition to the Black community to galvanize support from white voters, New York's mayoral candidates campaigned directly to Black voters for most of the Great Migration period. The fragmented party system in New York facilitated this positive interaction. Candidates for mayor had to win primary elections by building consensus and alliances among the smaller subparties and political clubs, described above. Further, once candidates passed the party primaries, they had to contend with an arrangement that allowed individuals to simultaneously compete on the ballot under the banner of multiple political parties. In some instances, mayors flip-flopped on civil rights issues after their election. On the whole, however, New York's mayoral candidates understood the potential political impact of the city's growing Black population and worked to include Black voters in their coalitions through their election campaigns.

From early in the Great Migration period, race was a political consideration in New York. For example, it featured prominently in John P. Mitchel's 1913 campaign for mayor of New York City. Mitchel ran as an independent Democrat and fusion candidate against the Tammany Hall candidate, Edward McCall. Tammany Hall sought to weaken Mitchel's position with Black voters by accusing him of being racist, like the newly inaugurated Democratic President Woodrow Wilson. Tammany also argued that fusion mayoral administrations of the past had failed to share patronage with Black New Yorkers at the same rate as Tammany administrations. Mitchel responded to the attacks with a campaign directed at Black voters. He took positions against segregation and promised to "appoint New Yorkers to government positions without regard to race or color" (Scheiner 1965: 207). Black New Yorkers supported Mitchel's candidacy in spite of the attacks from Tammany Hall. He won the election and held the office from 1914 to 1917.

Mitchel made good on his promises to Black voters over the course of his term in office. For example, he appointed Black people to positions in the police department and encouraged them to apply for jobs in the fire department.[9] Because the small number of Black people working in the Harlem hospital was a point of contention for many years, Mitchel appointed Black interns to positions there. Most notably, he appointed Dr. Eugene P. Roberts to the board of education (Lewinson 1974: 66). In addition to providing jobs, Mitchel created space for the citizens of Harlem—which was the center of the Black community by this time—to express their concerns about various issues. He responded in ways that indicated his understanding of and support for their positions. When the Black community complained about scenes from the 1915 movie *The Birth of a Nation*, he accepted their suggestion to prevent some parts of the movie from airing in the city. Although Tammany kept working to portray Mitchel as a racist, leaders in the Black community liked him. Yet despite support from Black voters, Mitchel could not overcome the strength of the Tammany machine.

John Hylan, the Democratic Party candidate, beat Mitchel in his mayoral reelection bid (Scheiner 1965: 210). Hylan fashioned himself as the candidate of poor and working-class people. He was attentive to Black interests as a candidate for mayor, and his campaign included outreach to Black voters in Harlem (Lewinson 1974: 66). He articulated a belief that there should be no "distinctions on account of race, creed or color, through either governmental agencies and any other agency" (Scheiner 1965: 210). He also noted his opposition to the Ku Klux Klan (KKK). In the end, Hylan won the 1917 election with about 27 percent of the Black vote.

For Hylan's 1921 mayoral reelection campaign, Ferdinand Q. Morton—the leader of the UCD and a migrant from Macon, Mississippi—advised him to continue outreach to the Black community. In talks with Black voters, Hylan touted that "civic rights and privileges of colored citizens ha[d] been fully and impartially recognized by the city" during his mayoral administration (Scheiner 1965: 210). As mayor, he had also raised money for the Urban League, and he promised to give the UCD a more prominent position in the "regular" Democratic Party dealings. His support in Black areas increased dramatically over the 1917 mayoral contest, with more than 70 percent of Black voters choosing to support him in the 1921 election (Lewinson 1974: 59).

But Hylan was inconsistent in his delivery of his 1921 campaign promises to Black voters. Although he kept the promises to appoint Black people to city positions, the jobs were limited and mostly reserved for Black people in middle-class circles. Additionally, Hylan had promised to make the UCD part of the white party organization but failed to keep his word after the election (Katznelson 1973: 71). Mayor Hylan lost the 1925 Democratic Party primary election to James J. Walker but decided to continue to campaign for mayor anyway.

The campaign issues of importance to the Black community in the 1925 election were public transportation fares, the presence of Black doctors and interns in Harlem's hospital, the appointment of Black judges to the municipal bench, and patronage through access to city jobs, including the police and fire departments.[10] Walker, a Tammany Democrat, campaigned for Black votes in the general election on the basis of increased access to patronage for the Black community. Walker argued that it would be easier to get benefits by working inside the machine than it would be to get them by fighting it. One of the city's Black newspapers, the *New York Amsterdam News*, was leery of Walker and the Democratic Party and encouraged Black voters to support his Republican opponent instead.[11] Walker won the election by a wide margin, but mostly without support from Black voters.[12]

Once elected, Walker used his influence to help with issues of importance to the Black community. For example, he worked with Fred Moore—a migrant from Washington, D.C., and alderman—to establish a medical center in North Harlem (Greenberg 1997: 95). Walker pledged to reorganize the Harlem Hospital to include more Black staff. He kept promises to increase the number of Black political appointees to various government positions, beginning with the reappointment of Morton to the Civil Service Commission. He also increased the number of Black people working in city jobs, from 247 to 2,275.

Walker resigned as mayor in September 1932 amid an investigation of widespread corruption within the Tammany organization. Joseph V. McKee and John P. O'Brien served as acting mayors after Walker's term. McKee, who was president of the board of aldermen, held the position of mayor until a special election occurred to fill the seat. O'Brien won the special election to finish Walker's term but was not reelected to the position in the 1933 regular election.

The 1933 mayoral campaign was the beginning of a set of challenges for Tammany Hall that would last through the rest of the decade. First, the party was still dealing with the negative effects of the investigation into its involvement with corruption and other illegal activities. Second, two Democratic candidates—McKee and O'Brien—split the Democratic Party vote (Furniss 1969: 115). Third, Congressman La Guardia was popular among Black leadership circles and running as a liberal reform candidate. La Guardia received a number of important Black endorsements in the campaign, including those of W. E. B. Du Bois and Oscar De Priest.[13] De Priest—himself a migrant living in Chicago, and the only Black member of the U.S. Congress—told New Yorkers that he was supporting La Guardia on the basis of his actions while a member of Congress. He shared that La Guardia had fought for anti-lynching legislation and had helped De Priest in his encounters with southern congressmen.[14] La Guardia won the mayoral contest of 1933 with large shares of the Black vote, especially in Harlem.[15]

Following his election to office, La Guardia remained popular in the Black community due to a number of actions. He aided in the appointment of Black New Yorkers to government positions by requiring that city officials follow strict guidelines—which were already in place—that prohibited discrimination in hiring. Further, he shared patronage through his appointment powers. La Guardia appointed two Black judges—Myles A. Paige and Jane Bolin—to benches in the city (Lewinson 1974: 72). In 1934, La Guardia heeded demands from the Black community to force the police commissioner's resignation after sustained charges of mistreatment.[16]

La Guardia did well in Black neighborhoods in his reelection campaigns of 1937 and 1941. During his terms as mayor, he continued to do work that benefited Black communities. In the early 1940s, he worked to decrease discrimination in defense industry hiring. While leaders in the civil rights community prepared for the 1941 March on Washington, which was subsequently called off, La Guardia worked to create the anti-discrimination policy that became the foundation of President Franklin Roosevelt's Executive Order 8802 to ban discrimination in war industries (Capeci 1977: 11). Further, La Guardia used the new executive order as the basis for an anti-discrimination policy in New York City's hiring practices. Reflecting on his progress for the 1941 campaign, La Guardia said, "My administration and myself have not treated Harlem any different than any other section of the city, but we have insisted on giving Harlem what any other section gets" (Capeci 1977: 9). La Guardia decided not to run for reelection in 1945, which left the field open for reformers and Tammany Hall candidates.

Following the La Guardia administration, Tammany faced a major problem in its outreach to Black voters. As mayor, La Guardia had been building his popularity in Black communities for the past twelve years and, in effect, conditioning Black voters to vote against Tammany Hall and the Democratic Party in local elections. William O'Dwyer was Tammany Hall's mayoral candidate as it sought to reestablish a foothold in New York City politics with the 1945 election. Recognizing the potential impact of the Black voting bloc in this contest, O'Dwyer and the Democratic Party decided to engage a leader in the Black community who could help them win support from Black voters. O'Dwyer appointed J. Raymond Jones as one of his campaign managers. Jones was a Black migrant from the U.S. Virgin Islands, who would come to be known as "the Harlem Fox." While Tammany was strategizing to return to power in the mayor's seat, the reform candidates split their votes. O'Dwyer won the 1945 election on the regular Democratic Party line with some help from smaller parties. Thanks to Jones, he enjoyed strong majorities in Harlem (Garrett 1961: 300).[17]

But by the next mayoral election, in 1949, O'Dwyer had mixed ratings among Black New Yorkers because of his positions on segregated housing and police brutality in the city (Biondi 2003: 209). Chief among his critics during the election was Harlem's very popular congressman, Powell. He rebuked and attempted to punish O'Dwyer for his support of Stuyvesant Town, a public-private housing and redevelopment partnership between the city government and the Metropolitan Life Insurance Company. Although the housing was supposed to be available to veterans and their families, the Metropolitan Life Insurance Company denied Black veterans' requests for housing. Powell believed that the mayor should take steps to ensure the fair treatment of potential Black tenants. To this end, Powell invited Mayor O'Dwyer's opponent to speak to the very large Black congregation of his Abyssinian Baptist Church without extending the mayor the same courtesy.[18]

In the later part of his mayoral administration, O'Dwyer also faced protests from the Brooklyn and New York State branches of the National Association for the Advancement of Colored People (NAACP). They charged that he was indirectly responsible for the rogue behavior of law enforcement officials because of his limited response to police murders of Black New Yorkers during his administration. Despite these problems with Black leaders, he got the endorsement of the *New York Age*, a Black newspaper, which cited his previous actions and uncertainty about the potential actions of his opponents as the reason for its support.[19] In the end, O'Dwyer ran well in the Black community and won reelection in 1949.

Amid problems in his personal and professional life, O'Dwyer resigned as mayor to take an ambassadorship to Mexico in 1950. His resignation made Vincent Impellitteri—the president of the city council—the mayor of New York City. In a special election later that year, Impellitteri ran for mayor as an independent candidate. He campaigned with a commitment to treat New York's Black community without prejudice. Further, he conveyed understanding and concern for many of the issues of importance to Black voters. On the issue of jobs in city government, he promised to appoint a Black person as a full commissioner in the city administration.[20] He expressed support for open housing in the city, which had been a topic of debate since the opening of the Stuyvesant Town housing community during the O'Dwyer administration.[21] Impellitteri won the 1950 election.

The issues with policing in New York City that had proved problematic in O'Dwyer's administration continued during Impellitteri's term. His response to these problems caused difficulties in his interactions with the Black community. In 1950, after a police officer killed a Black war veteran, Impellitteri showed no remorse for the murder and did not apologize to members of the Black community for what had happened (Biondi 2003: 192). When he sought reelection, the Black community declined to support him.

Impellitteri's opponent in the 1953 Democratic primary election was Robert F. Wagner Jr., who had been borough president and a member of the state assembly before running for mayor. During the primary election, Wagner made clear his positions on issues of importance to Black voters. He vowed to work for city laws that would prevent discrimination in public and private housing options.[22] Wagner beat Impellitteri in the Democratic primary election. Following the primary election, Wagner acknowledged the importance of Black voters to his victory: "Without the United Citizens Committee, the Harlem Independent Citizens Committee, Hulan Jack, Anne Arnold Hedgeman, and Thelma Berlack Boozer— all of whom carried me on to victory and helped immeasurably—I could not have won this primary battle."[23]

In the general election, Wagner continued his campaigning to Black New Yorkers by pledging to increase access to housing, jobs, and grocery options. In a meeting with leaders of the Black and Puerto Rican communities, he told them that one of his first acts as mayor would be to "see that there would be an integration at the planning level of government of those who too often get bypassed."[24] He also promised to improve grocery conditions and access to food options in Harlem. Large numbers of Black voters supported Wagner in the 1953 campaign (McNickle 1993: 107), and he won in Harlem by a 3–1 margin.[25]

Wagner faced criticism from the Black community on some issues after becoming mayor and, in some instances, responded to their concerns. People in Harlem became upset about delays in the renovations of Harlem Hospital that lasted nearly two years. By the time the hospital was finished, Black New Yorkers were so jaded by the process that they questioned whether Wagner and Tammany Hall had strategically delayed the hospital's reopening to prevent problems in an upcoming election.[26] In another incident, Wagner became the subject of protests from the Black community for failing to appoint Black New Yorkers to city jobs. He responded by appointing a Black woman as his mayoral assistant. He also worked with the city council to pass the Sharkey-Brown-Isaacs bill, an anti-discrimination in housing law that was among the first of its kind in the nation. Although there were some problems with implementation, Democrats believed that the Sharkey-Brown-Isaacs bill was a step in the right direction. Wagner remained in office until 1965.

Black Voters as the BOP in Elections

In Chapter 1, I argue that politicians' interactions with Black voters would have varied on the basis of not only the spatial distribution of Black people and the rules for election to office in the city but also the degree of party cohesion. New York's political environment was fragmented in at least three important ways that shaped the city's politics and the ways in which Black New Yorkers interacted with their government:

1. The city's population was very large and included a great diversity of people from different ethnic and racial groups. The Black population grew rapidly during the Great Migration period, but, even with the growth, Black voters were a relatively small percentage of the city's overall population when compared to Detroit and Chicago.
2. The city's political apparatuses for representation were separated and organized by boroughs. Each borough had a separate party organization, with its own leaders and rules of engagement. This arrangement meant that Black voters could not leverage the strength of their entire voting bloc for local positions other than mayor.
3. The major political parties were further divided into factions and political clubs that often took opposing positions on issues.

I have some reasons to expect that politicians would not have been attentive to the requests of the Black community. For one,

TABLE 4.2. BALANCE OF POWER POTENTIAL, NEW YORK CITY MAYORAL ELECTIONS, 1917–1965		
Black voting age population (BVAP) estimate		
100% of BVAP	67% of BVAP	50% of BVAP
6 of 15 elections	4 of 15 elections	3 of 15 elections
Source: Compiled by the author.		

the Black community was relatively small as a percentage of the overall population for most of the period. However, I also have reasons to expect that politicians would have sought support from Black voters during the period. The parties' division into such small regional and factional groups meant that candidates had to build coalitions to win local elections. One of the other factors I outline as important in white politicians' and parties' political decision making is whether the Black population was the BOP in elections. I assume that parties and politicians would have been more concerned with meeting Black voters' needs if they believed the Black voters might tip the electoral balance for or against them in an election.

To determine whether Black voters in New York were the BOP for mayoral elections from 1915 to 1965, I compare three estimates of the Black voting age population (BVAP) to the margin of victory in elections. When I compare 100 percent of the BVAP to numerical margins of victory in mayoral elections, Black voters could have been the BOP in six instances, or 40 percent of elections. When I reduce the BOP estimate to 67 percent of the BVAP, Black voters could have been the BOP in four of the fifteen elections, or 27 percent of the time. Finally, in three elections, or 20 percent of the time, Black voters could have been the BOP when I consider half of the BVAP. These figures are illustrated in Table 4.2.

One of the foundational assumptions of this book is that politicians would behave in ways that were beneficial to Black voters when they believed that Black voters were the BOP in an electoral situation. Campaigning to Black voters was important to New York's mayoral candidates for at least two reasons. First, although it was clear that Black voters were not

Figure 4.1. Black women at a polling place in New York or New Jersey, November 1957. (Photo by Thomas J. O'Halloran for U.S. News and World Report. Library of Congress Collection.

singularly the BOP in elections, they demonstrated that they could be very important partners in a coalition of voters. The Black community expressed its agency and willingness to participate in the political process through independent political clubs and third parties. Black voters published newspapers and pamphlets, organized themselves through their churches and civic organizations, and agitated for attention to their issues through political clubs and third parties. Figure 4.1 is a photo of Black women voters in 1957. Black voters' significance in the electorate would increase as the Black electorate grew through migration and natural expansion. Second, and more importantly, the divisions in the city's political parties and system of fusion politics meant that Black voters could be influential even when the BVAP was not large enough to change the outcomes of elections by itself.

In each of the mayoral elections under consideration here, the candidates did campaign on issues of importance to Black voters. They understood that Black voters could vote strategically, as a bloc to support candidates who represented their interests. New York City's mayoral candidates may have differed in the frequency and degree to which they kept their promises to the Black community, but they all sought to engage the Black community for political support.

Black Political Office Holders

Black New Yorkers' ability to hold public office was limited by the distribution of the Black population throughout the city and the rules for election to office. Because each borough had a separate political apparatus, it was difficult for Black people to exercise the full potential of their voting bloc in citywide contests (Biondi 2003: 208). Further, Black New Yorkers often struggled to get fair representation in the state assembly because white politicians created gerrymandered districts. Dividing the predominantly Black populations of Harlem and Brooklyn between surrounding white districts reduced the likelihood that Black people could be elected to office, even when they had clear majorities in communities.

Black New Yorkers encountered the same problems when they tried to earn leadership posts in the political parties. For much of the period, their options were to start their own political clubs or to hope for a position in the Black submachines of the Democratic Party. These posts were either appointed by the white area leaders or by the machine-appointed Black community leaders (Biondi 2003; Lewinson 1974; Walton 1972). In spite of these structural challenges, Black New Yorkers were elected to office at various levels of government throughout the Great Migration. By 1965, Black New Yorkers were able to have greater influence in political parties and to be elected to office at rates commensurate with their share of the population.

Between 1915 and 1965, forty Black New Yorkers won election to positions in the city government, the state assembly, or the U.S. Congress.[27] The number of Black officials elected to political office increased over the course of the Great Migration. Twenty-one of them—or more than half—were southern migrants, and six of them were West Indian. These numbers are commensurate with the likely number of migrants in the overall population of Black people in New York. However, it is noteworthy that so many participants in the Great Migration were able to get elected to political office so soon after their relocation. More migrants were elected to the state legislature than to municipal office or to Congress. That more of them served in the state legislature than the city council is consistent with my expectations about the rules for elected office: it has always been easier for particular racial and ethnic groups to elect representatives from homogenous, residence-based districts.

Only three of New York's Black elected officials were women, and none of the women was a migrant. Bessie A. Buchanan, whose parents migrated to New York from Virginia before she was born, became the first Black woman in the state assembly in 1955. She was followed in the state legislature by Shirley Chisholm and Constance Baker Motley, both elected in 1964. In 1968, Chisholm would go on to become the first Black woman elected to Congress. No Black woman would serve in the city council until 1974, when Mary Pinkett was elected from Brooklyn. New York had fewer women (three) elected to public office than did Detroit (five). Both cities had more women in public office than Chicago, which had just one.

In the rest of this section, I discuss Black New Yorkers' election to political office at the state and local levels. I describe the policy concerns of the Black elected officials in the state legislature and the city council. Along the way, I also highlight the Black elected officials who were migrants. Where they existed, I describe legislative issues related to the migration.

Black New Yorkers in the State Legislature

Because much of the legislative decision making on New York City issues happened in the state assembly, a seat in the state legislature was more important to New Yorkers than election to the city council (Lewinson 1974). As in Detroit and Chicago, political gerrymandering prevented Black people from being nominated for and elected to political office at rates that were commensurate with their population growth during the Great Migration. Eventually, however, the numbers of Black people in communities grew so large that parties recognized that they would have to nominate Black candidates to win elections. Black New Yorkers also gained power in formal political organizations during this period, which put them in a better position to determine party strategy and nomination decisions.

Johnson was the first Black person elected to the state legislature in New York. A migrant from North Carolina, he ran and was elected as a Republican with strong support from one of the early Black Republican political clubs. Johnson served for two years at a time when assembly elections occurred annually. During his short tenure, he helped secure the passage of several bills. One of his major accomplishments was strengthening New York's first civil rights bill so it extended civil rights protections to include "places of public accommodation, amusement and resort."[28] Also noteworthy was Johnson's effort to establish a Negro division in the State Employment Bureau for New Yorkers.[29] This goal would have been especially important to migrants, who were coming to New York with the expectation that they would be able to find employment.

In New York, Black state legislators' priorities were similar to those in Michigan and Illinois. Generally, they were concerned with racial discrimination in various parts of life, including but not limited to housing, employment, and interactions with corporations and government entities. There are two noteworthy differences in the legislative priorities of Black New Yorkers in the state assembly when compared to their Black counterparts in Detroit and Chicago: (1) they paid additional attention to issues of crime and law enforcement and (2) on a number of occasions, they introduced bills to provide equal access to insurance policies. As people continued to flow into New York City through migration, they also fought for an increased amount of elected political representation to reflect the growth in the population. In the following section, I describe their attempts to secure legislation in these areas.

Broader Concerns of Black Officials in the State Legislature

Fair housing was a leading concern in New York City throughout the period of interest, especially as the Black population grew during the Great Migration. Black New Yorkers experienced difficulty finding housing that accepted Black residents. When they did find housing, they were often forced to pay exorbitant rents or higher-than-average mortgage rates. In 1929, Lamar Perkins and Frances E. Rivers—migrants from Georgia and Oklahoma, respectively—won election to the state assembly. In an interview with the *New York Amsterdam News*, they remarked that emergency rent control would be their first priority.[30] Perkins introduced legislation that would allow municipal court judges to grant tenants more time to find alternative housing before they were evicted.[31] Rivers went on to sponsor legislation that would require landlords to maintain their properties by making repairs in a timely fashion rather than forcing tenants to live in subpar housing units.[32] In 1950, Joseph Pinkney—a migrant from South Carolina—recognized that problems with housing were still top-of-mind for many New Yorkers. He vowed that affordable housing would be at the top of his political agenda: "I feel that the method used in selecting tenants for low cost housing is working against Negro veterans and families who are within the income bracket and that will be one of my first duties—to investigate why."[33]

The New York State Assembly considered fair-housing legislation for many of the years during the period of the Great Migration. In 1955, legislators reached an important milestone when the first of the state's Metcalf-Baker laws passed. This new housing legislation was a very important development in the fight for fair housing. The laws were the product of a working relationship between George Metcalf, a white Republican state senator, and Bertram Baker, a Black Democratic assemblyman from Brooklyn. The first of these laws prohibited racial discrimination in places that had more than ten dwelling units and were financed with government-backed loans, such as Federal Housing Administration (FHA) and Veterans Administration (VA) loans.[34] Following their initial legislation, Metcalf and Baker continued working together to strengthen other parts of housing laws in New York State in subsequent years.

Another major concern for Black New Yorkers was employment discrimination. State Assemblyman William T. Andrews, who was originally from South Carolina, introduced two bills to change the employment landscape for Black workers in 1940: the first bill sought to remove state protections from unions that engaged in racial discrimination, and the second bill sought civil and criminal charges against members of unions who discriminated on the basis of race.[35] In the following legislative session, Andrews worked with two other members of the assembly—Daniel Burrows, a migrant from Virginia, and Hulan Jack, a West Indian immigrant—to establish the New York State War Council Committee on Discrimination in Employment.[36] This committee would serve as the foundation for employment discrimination law in the state.

In 1945, New York became the first state to legislate against discrimination in employment because of race, creed, color, or national origin. The Ives-Quinn law went into effect as the legislation that had created the Fair Employment Practices Committee (FEPC) was about to end, without a guarantee that the laws would be extended in Congress.[37] With support from Black state legislators, the law established the State Committee Against Discrimination.[38] But Black New Yorkers were not always successful in their attempts to win employment protections. Assemblyman James E. Stephens, a native New Yorker, introduced legislation that would make it illegal for public utilities to discriminate on the basis of a resident's race. When the legislation failed, more than one thousand people met to vent their frustrations about Republicans' role defeating the legislation.[39]

Interactions with police and law enforcement officials troubled Black city dwellers for much of the period of interest. Their fears were expressed in the legislation they introduced at the state and local levels. In 1938, Assemblyman Robert Justice—a migrant from North Carolina—introduced legislation to decriminalize a popular form of gambling in the city. Recognizing that "playing the numbers" created the potential for harassment of Black New Yorkers who sought to play the lottery, Justice successfully moved a bill through the state assembly to prevent the arrest of individuals caught playing.[40] In the same year, Justice sought to limit police officers' ability to search individuals in their homes or businesses without a warrant.[41]

Black members of the state assembly were also concerned about representation and the fair apportionment of electoral districts. They recognized the changes in the city's population that stemmed from the Great Migration. Long before *Baker v. Carr* and the ruling that all citizens in a democracy should have equal access to the ballot, Black New Yorkers argued that their numerical strength was such that more of them should have been nominated for and elected to political offices. Battles about representation took place on two fronts: within party organizations and through legislative actions. The level of representation in the state legislature—in the state senate, especially—was not reflective of the changes in the size of the Black population. Politicians frequently drew lines in suspicious ways, and Black elected officials knew it.

In 1935, led by Governor Herbert Lehman, New York Democrats drafted legislation to redraw lines for the state legislature. Stephens (from Harlem) and Andrews (originally from South Carolina) voiced their opposition to this legislation from their own party. They argued that the new lines would contribute to a lack of Black representation by reducing the number of individuals elected from Harlem. Stephens commented on the floor of the legislature that the bill "will never pass until we get proper Negro representation in the senate."[42] Stephens and Andrews broke from the Democratic ranks when they voted. The bill did not pass, and Democrats were forced to reconsider their reapportionment plans.[43]

The drive to expand representation and elect a Black person to the state senate continued. By 1952, the Twenty-First State Senate District's population was mostly Black and Puerto Rican. However, the district was represented by a white Tammany Democrat. Believing that the time was right to win a seat in the state senate, Black New Yorkers created the Non-Partisan Committee to Elect a Negro State Senator. They rejected calls from party leaders—white and Black—to keep the white incumbent. Instead, the group backed Julius Archibald, an immigrant from Trinidad, for the seat.[44] Archibald went on to win the primary and general elections in 1952 and served two two-year terms (Lewinson 1974: 86). He was later defeated in a primary election contest by James L. Watson, another Black elected official from New York, who served in the position until 1963.

In contrast to the citizens of Michigan and Illinois, evidence shows that New Yorkers were very focused on ending discrimination in insurance markets. Black elected officials' concerns included the unwillingness of some companies to write insurance policies, the poor treatment of Black policyholders, and the inflated costs of insurance for Black consumers. In 1935, Stephens secured legislation to ensure that "no insurance corporation shall reject any applicant for a policy or refuse any applicant a policy after it has been applied for, solely by reason of the applicant's being of African descent."[45] Later, Buchanan worked with a colleague in the state senate to prevent insurance companies' practices of refusing to sell automobile and fire policies in Harlem.[46] Other Black assemblymen, including Elijah Crump and Thomas Dickens—both of whom were migrants—also introduced measures to end insurance discrimination.[47]

Legislative Concerns of Black Migrants

For the most part, migrants faced the same problems as native New Yorkers. Most of the legislative concerns of the migrants elected to the New York State Assembly mirrored those of their northern-born counterparts. In a few instances, elected officials who were not migrants themselves worked with migrant lawmakers to express concern for the plight of people moving to New York from the South. State legislators were very often concerned about the working conditions of migrants and sought to establish rules that governed their well-being while in the state.[48] For example, through his work as the secretary of the Joint Legislative Committee in the state senate, native New Yorker James Watson sought protections for Black agricultural workers who came to

New York for seasonal work in 1958. One bill would require farms to begin "correction of slovenly and often non-existent payrolls."[49]

In the following legislative session, Watson worked on a bill with Lloyd Dickens, a migrant from Oklahoma, to guarantee a minimum wage to migrant workers in New York State. The legislation proposed that farmers would pay workers one dollar per hour and that any worker who made more than fifteen dollars per year must be eligible for the state's unemployment benefits.[50] In 1964, Assemblyman Ivan Warner sought to close three upstate New York migrant camps for unsafe conditions. He described the conditions to the *Amsterdam News* as "a complete disgrace, in which human beings are living in conditions worse than animals and operators of the camps are flagrantly disregarding the laws of the state."[51]

Black Elected Officials in Local Elected Positions

New York's main governing body, the board of alderman (later the city council), had fourteen Black members between 1915 and 1965; eight of them were migrants. Until 1937, the board of aldermen consisted of seventy individuals elected to represent residential districts throughout the city in two-year terms. The local electoral system changed after a state constitutional convention in 1937, which established a city council of twenty-six members who were elected to four-year terms. The changes also included a system of proportional representation. Seats in the city council were apportioned on the basis of voter turnout in the election, with each borough entitled to at least one seat in the council. Rather than running in just one part of the city, office seekers ran across the five boroughs. Each voter in the city was supposed to rank all candidates for city council in numerical order. Candidates with seventy-five thousand votes were assured a seat on the city council. Remaining candidates would be seated in rank order for their borough. If six seats were available for Manhattan, the six individuals with the largest vote shares would each win a place on the council (Hamilton 1992: 115).

The stated goal of proportional representation was to increase access to the city council for underrepresented groups. However, a four-year lapse in Black representation on the city council followed the shift to proportional representation. Black New Yorkers regained representation in the city council with the 1941 election of Adam Clayton Powell. Powell, a native New Yorker and eventually one of the most important figures in the city's political history, won election to the city council with a strategy of "bullet voting."[52] In this strategy, individuals would assign their votes to just one candidate. This tactic deprived other candidates of the benefit of getting support by being listed second or third on a voter's ballot. Powell worked with the American Labor Party and religious and civic organizations to instruct Harlem voters in strategic voting. In the end, he won his seat in the council with sixty-four thousand votes (Hamilton 1992).

Local Legislative Concerns

Black New Yorkers in municipal elected positions had a number of legislative concerns. For the most part, migrants who were elected to positions in city government had the same political concerns as northern-born Black elected officials. Further, many of the local issues paralleled the concerns articulated by Black elected officials in the state legislature. Anti-discrimination was a broad concern at both levels of government. Elected officials at both levels worked to increase access to various accommodations in the city. However, local government officeholders did express specific concerns about access to adequate housing and health care in the city as well as crime and law enforcement.

In 1915, Dr. Charles H. Roberts, a dentist and a migrant from South Carolina, became the first Black person elected to the board of aldermen.[53] A Republican, Roberts represented the Twenty-Seventh Aldermanic District (AD). During his time as an alderman, Roberts worked on a number of issues, including a fight to keep a police precinct in Harlem and attempts to strengthen the consequences for armed robbery. His most notable accomplishment was the securement of funding for a bathhouse and recreation facility in his district.[54] He first advocated for the bathhouse in 1920, describing his vision of a place for "the comfort, care, and well-being of Harlem children."[55] It evolved into a larger-scale project that would be located in Harlem but open to the entire community, regardless of race.

Adequate housing was an issue in Harlem over the entire course of the Great Migration. Housing was limited and overpriced for Black people settling in the city. Landlords also often did not maintain healthy spaces for Black tenants. Once they were elected to city positions, Black folks worked to improve housing conditions. When one of his constituents complained in 1924 that she was forced to live in unsanitary conditions, Alderman John W. Smith—a migrant from Virginia—wrote to the board of health and to the Tenement House Department for a remedy. Although the departments had failed to respond directly to the tenant, they heeded the alderman's request to help her.[56]

Virginia native Earl Brown made housing one of his top priorities in the 1950s. In the wake of the migration's second wave, Brown asked the city council to consider investigating housing shortages caused by migration. Brown argued that the "extended demolition of housing taking place under current programs, and the curtailment of Federal funds, would deprive the city of accommodations for 180,000 low-income persons."[57] Later in the period, Brown worked with two white city councilmen on antidiscrimination legislation for private housing. The focus of the bill in its early stages was the planned segregation of the Stuyvesant Town housing development. The resulting legislation—the Sharkey-Brown-Isaacs law—built on the Metcalf-Baker law from the state legislature to specify that discrimination in private housing was illegal.[58] Over time, the council revised the legislation to prohibit discrimination in various parts of city life. For instance, later iterations of the bill prohibited charities in the city from receiving funds if they discriminated against children on the basis of race.

The condition of the Harlem Hospital and access to medical facilities was another issue of concern to Black aldermen and city councilmen. In 1921, George W. Harris worked with a committee of his constituents to argue for greater Black representation on the hospital staff. Harris estimated that half of the people using the hospital facilities were Black; therefore, Black people should be represented in the positions of surgeon, physician, and nurse.[59] As the migration continued and brought more people into the city, concerns grew about the well-being of "people arriving in the city from warmer climates." The city's health commissioner warned that the rate of death was higher for the people of North Harlem. In response, Moore—an alderman and migrant from Washington, D.C.—worked with Mayor Walker to open a medical center in the burgeoning Black community in 1929.[60]

New Yorkers' interactions with the police were complicated: they wanted to limit police interference in their lives but needed officers' assistance with keeping peace in their communities. In 1953, City Councilman Brown succeeded in implementing a rule change that allowed the city council's Rules Committee to investigate allegations of the unwanted use of force and abuse by police.[61] The legislation also worked to give the committee the power to investigate complaints about the police and police training practices. By 1959, parts of New York City were experiencing an uptick in crime. Some of the crimes were attributed to the presence of juvenile gangs in the city. City Councilmen Brown and J. Daniel Diggs—a migrant from North Carolina—worked with the mayor to confront this problem. Diggs, who represented the Bedford-Stuyvesant section of Brooklyn, proposed a 10:00 P.M. curfew for young people in the city. Brown went even further in response to a string of four murders in the span of one week. He told the *New York Daily News* that the problem of juvenile crime must end, "even if it would require more resolute police action to accomplish it."[62]

Black New Yorkers in Congress

Because the political boundaries were drawn to inhibit Black political power, Black New Yorkers did not achieve descriptive representation at the congressional level until 1945. Harlem voters elected Adam Clayton Powell to Congress from New York's Twenty-Second Congressional District. Powell was a native New

Yorker who came to prominence through his post as the pastor of the Abyssinian Baptist Church in Harlem. Powell would be the only Black representative of New York's massive Black population until Shirley Chisholm—a native New Yorker with West Indian parents—won election to Congress from Brooklyn's Twelfth Congressional District in 1972.

Before Powell got elected to office, a number of Black New Yorkers attempted to win the congressional seat, usually running from outside the Democratic Party organization. They failed because successful gerrymandering of Black residential areas prevented a critical mass of Black voters in a single congressional district. In 1924, Dr. Charles Roberts, the city's first Black alderman, became the first Black person nominated to run for Congress in New York City when he won the nomination of the Republican Party.[63] Roberts ran against a white Democrat and lost the election by just 7,829 votes.[64] Other Black candidates, including Edward A. Johnson and Hubert T. Delaney, were unsuccessful in their bids for office, despite winning the support of Black voters in Harlem.

In 1942, New York's state legislature completed a long and contentious reapportionment process and settled on lines that would create an all-Black congressional seat for the 1944 election. Powell's opponent in the 1944 contest was a Black woman and migrant named Sara Pelman Speaks. Speaks, a Republican teacher and social worker, had won the 1937 Republican primary election to represent the 21AD in the state legislature. Although she lost in the 1937 general election, she remained active in politics. In 1944, she and the Republican Party argued that she was the best qualified to represent Harlem in Congress. However, Powell added his name to the Republican primary ballot. He also filed for a place on the ballots of the Democratic Party and the American Labor Party. Powell won the primary elections of all three political organizations. He went on to win the general election of 1944 and become the first Black representative in the U.S. Congress from the state of New York.

As a member of Congress, Powell was limited in what he

could accomplish as one of only two Black members. In the beginning of his tenure, he concerned himself with symbolic positions that spoke to the concerns of his constituents and of Black Americans in general. For example, he argued for the establishment of a permanent FEPC, which had been temporarily created by Roosevelt's executive order in 1941. Working in conjunction with the NAACP, he employed the use of "Powell Amendments." These legislative riders sought to amend congressional legislation to prevent segregation in the execution of federal laws (Hamilton 1992; Lewinson 1974). His fight against segregation also happened in the Capitol itself, when he encouraged his staff to use previously segregated accommodations, such as the cafeteria and the barbershop (Lewinson 1974).

Conclusion

Political parties and elected officials in New York did not view Black voters as the BOP because the Black community alone could not change the outcome of elections. Further, in my calculations, they did not represent the BOP—as I use the term—in most of the mayoral elections from 1915 to 1965. Although they were not able to change the outcome of the election as a singular group, they were important as coalition partners in a large and diverse electorate. Mayoral candidates and political parties recognized them as a significant part of the political landscape. Mayoral candidates between 1915 and 1965 routinely paid attention to Black voters and sought to secure their support.

Black people were able to get elected to office relatively early in New York. Slightly more than half—52 percent—of the Black elected officials in New York were migrants from the South. Early on, Black people in the city formed political clubs that represented their interests. Black political clubs registered, educated, and mobilized voters at the beginning of the period. As the migration continued, more and more Black citizens were able to get elected to office. Along with the growth of the Black population over the period, redistricting helped increase the numbers of Black people who were elected to office. Eventually, so many Black people lived in some of the legislative districts that Black political leaders deemed separate Black clubs unnecessary. By the late 1950s, Black candidates for office ran from various political parties, and some Black politicians had ascended to leadership in these parties.

As legislators, migrants did not show a distinct difference in their attention to issues from their northern-born counterparts. Black elected officials brought issues to the forefront that might not have been voiced by individuals outside the Black community. For example, Black New Yorkers felt the shortages in available and affordable housing because they experienced them and because the Great Migration put stress on New York City's housing stock. Individuals moving to New York came with the expectation that they would be able to find employment. As a result, Black people who held elected office were very concerned about discrimination in housing and employment opportunities. Over the period, they were able to work with allies in the state legislature and the city council to make New York State a leader in legislation that protected all people from discrimination when seeking housing and employment.

5

Chicago

In Black politics, Chicago—sometimes referred to as "the Political Capital of Black America" (Harris 2012: 35)—is important for being a place where Black people held political office before they were able to do so in other northern cities. For many of the participants in the Great Migration, Chicago was the premier destination. This view was especially true for migrants coming north from Mississippi, Alabama, and Arkansas. Migration to Chicago began early, as Black folks went to work in the war industries. The national influence of the city's Black newspaper, the *Chicago Defender*, and word of mouth helped sustain migration to the city.

The 1910 Census reports the Black population of Chicago as 44,103, or about 2 percent of the city's total population. The Black population increased by more than 100 percent in the next two decades. By 1920, there were 109,458 Black Chicagoans. The number had jumped to 233,903 by the 1930 Census. Migration to Chicago slowed during the Great Depression, as it did for most cities. However, it did not stop, and the Black population had increased by 19 percent at the time of the 1940 Census. By 1950, Black Chicagoans were nearly half a million in number, at 492,635. They accounted for nearly 23 percent of the city's over-

TABLE 5.1. CHICAGO POPULATION, 1910–1970

Year	Total population	Black population	Percentage Black
1910	2,185,283	44,103	2.02%
1920	2,701,705	109,458	4.05%
1930	3,376,438	233,903	6.93%
1940	3,896,808	277,731	7.13%
1950	3,611,580	492,635	13.64%
1960	3,550,404	812,836	22.89%
1970	3,366,957	1,098,824	32.64%

Source: U.S. Census Bureau (1910–1970), *Censuses of the Population, Statistics for Illinois, Detailed Characteristics of the Population.* Compiled by the author.

all population by 1960 and were more than one million in total number by 1965. Table 5.1 shows the growth of the Chicago's Black population from 1910 to 1970.

Housing in Chicago was segregated, with ethnic groups living in separate parts of the city for most of the Great Migration era. This separation changed over time, as many white ethnic groups integrated into the broader white society during the period. But Black people in Chicago did not have the luxury of acceptance through assimilation. They were confined to the South Side of the city for the majority of the Great Migration period, regardless of their financial means or preferences. Eventually, their numbers grew so large that they began to spill over into parts of the city adjoining the South Side. This expansion led to clashes with their white neighbors in some instances. The changes in residential landscape also had political consequences, which I describe below.

The rest of this chapter discusses the political environment in Chicago, providing information about the city's political parties and rules for elected office. It then describes the relationship between Chicago's Black population and its mayoral candidates. Finally, it describes the formal political involvement of Black Chicagoans. In discussing the political interests of the full population of Black elected officials during the Great Migration period, I identify the Black elected officials who were migrants and consider whether they had political positions or policy foci that differed from those of their northern-born counterparts.

Political Environment

Elected officials in Illinois were required to reside in the state for five years before running for office. Terms in the state senate, the upper house in the state legislature, were complicated. Within a given decade, members of the state senate were elected to two four-year terms and one two-year term. Members of the Illinois General Assembly, the lower house of the state legislature, were elected to two-year terms from fifty-one senatorial districts. General assembly members were not subject to term limits. In the state's system of cumulative voting, Illinois citizens got three votes, which they could use to elect representatives to the lower house of the state legislature. This system allowed for strategic voting: voters could concentrate their three votes on one individual or spread their votes across multiple candidates. For example, a voter could give all of his or her votes to candidate A; give two votes to candidate A and one vote to candidate B; or give one vote each to candidates A, B, and C.

During the Great Migration era, Chicago's mayor was arguably the most powerful politician in the state of Illinois, making local politics very important even beyond the confines of the city. The city is governed by the same strong mayor system, with a city council composed of single-member district representatives. At the beginning of the period, the city council was composed of seventy aldermen, with two people representing each of the thirty-five wards (Wilson 1960: 73). In 1923, the number of wards increased to fifty, but the number of aldermen decreased to one per ward, making for a fifty-member city council. The wards were small and usually represented a homogenous population of voters. Because of discriminatory housing policies in Chicago, most Black residents lived in the Second Ward. In 1910, the Second Ward was 37 percent Black and probably majority Black by 1915 (74). In the 1920 census, it was 70 percent Black.[1] The number of majority-Black political districts grew over time, such that there were eventually enough Black Chicagoans to elect city officials from multiple wards. By the end of the period, Black voters would hold majorities in the Second, Third, Fourth, Sixth, and Twentieth Wards.

Party Cohesion

Party control of the Chicago mayor's seat alternated between Republicans and Democrats until the 1930s, when Democrats permanently gained control of the city. Because intraparty factions were the foundation of political competition in the city, primary elections were often more important to determining who would become mayor than were the general elections. Sometimes, Black voters were the balance of power (BOP) in primary elections, which paved a path toward victory for mayoral candidates.

Mayoral candidates took diverse approaches to building coalitions, with some choosing to include Black voters as part of their strategy and others choosing to highlight race in negative ways to establish a coalition of white ethnic groups. At the beginning of the migration period, Republican candidates—especially William "Big Bill" Thompson—were more likely to recruit Black support to build their coalitions. By 1935, the Democratic Party was in control of the city and headed by a faction interested in making Black voters a part of the Democratic coalition. However, later in the period, Democrats expressed varying levels of concern about getting support from Black voters. Their stances varied from ignoring and disregarding Black voters to actively working to decrease the likelihood of voting in Black communities.

Both political parties created Black submachines to organize Black voters in the South Side wards rather than allow them to participate with white residents in what they referred to as the "regular" parties. The Black political organizations were active before the Great Migration began and continued to be through the 1970s (Gordon 1969; Grimshaw 1992; Walton 1972). Through the submachines, Black elected officials worked to ensure that their parties won the majority of votes in the precincts with large Black populations. As I discuss further below, the submachines were a bit of a blessing and a curse. They were helpful as a way to organize Black voters, but sometimes submachine leaders' loyalties were to their parties rather than to their constituents. In these instances, the political interactions and outcomes were less demanding of action on Black issues than they might have been without strict oversight from the parties.

Mayoral Party and Candidate Interactions

City Councilman Thompson, a Republican, was "one of the first politicians to court the Black vote actively" (Biles 1984: 89). His first major outreach came in the form of the city's first playground. As a member of the city council, Thompson advocated putting the equipment in his district, which included Chicago's Black neighborhood. He argued that race should not be a consideration in the location of the playground. Instead, Thompson argued, the city should consider putting the equipment in the ward with the most children. His attention to Black voters paid dividends when he decided to run for mayor from the city council. In the 1915 mayoral primary election, opposition from a rival faction in the Republican Party posed a serious threat to his bid for mayor. Support from Black voters, who were the BOP in Thompson's primary election victory, saved him. Again, in the 1919 primary, Black voters were critical in boosting Thompson's ability to win his party's nomination for mayor. He went on to win the 1919 mayoral general election.

Thompson was unable to run for reelection in 1923 because he was facing corruption charges. To spite the Republican Party, he encouraged Black voters to support the Democratic candidate, William Dever. Black Republican politicians, namely Oscar De Priest and Louis B. Anderson, also encouraged Black voters to support Dever because they were leery of the Republican mayoral candidate, Arthur C. Lueder (Schmidt 1989: 73). The percentage of Black Chicagoans voting for the Democratic mayoral candidate rose from 20 percent in 1919 to 53 percent in 1923. In return for their support, Dever made public statements about his intention to support Black Chicagoans. Just after the election, speaking to a group of two thousand Black delegates to the convention of the Negro Sanhedrin, a civic organization, "the mayor assured his audience that, so long as he was mayor, colored people in Chicago would be given justice and treated with equality."[2] He rewarded the Black community by giving patronage to his Black supporters (Gosnell 1967).

Dever's interactions with the Black community worsened during his administration. In particular, his approach to law enforcement in Black communities was problematic. He ordered the police to conduct a series of raids on South Side nightclubs in the name of prohibition. The publicly stated goal of the raids was to end prostitution and illicit activities in the city. However, many people in the Black community believed that the mayor's real intention was to end interracial socializing in Chicago. Relations between Mayor Dever and the Black community would reach their lowest point during his next mayoral campaign.

Dever's opponent in 1927 was Thompson, the former mayor. Democrats saw race-baiting as a way to unify their party when disparate groups of white ethnics needed a rallying issue (Schmidt 1989: 160). Further, Dever and the Democratic Party machine did not believe that the population of Black voters would be large enough to influence the outcome of the 1927 election. Therefore, Dever focused on unifying white voters in the Democratic Party and traded his previously positive interactions with Black voters for a more threatening position toward them. For example, Dever's supporters released campaign materials that took specific aim at the new migrants to Chicago. The literature included an illustration of Thompson as the conductor of a train from Georgia to Chicago. The caption read, "This train will start for Chicago, April 6, if Thompson is elected" (Bunche 1929: 78).

As he had in the past, Thompson campaigned for Black votes. Thompson highlighted Dever's law enforcement attacks on the South Side and denounced the racist rhetoric of his opponent's campaign. Black voters turned out to vote against the racism on display from Dever and the Democratic Party. Despite tremendous growth in the Black population at the time, the number of Black voters supporting Democrats in 1927 decreased by one-third from what it had been in 1923 (Schmidt 1989: 102). With tremendous support from the Black community, as had been critical in previous campaigns, Thompson won the general election.

Thompson's long career in politics ended after a successful challenge from Democrat Anton Cermak.[3] In the 1931 election, the number of voters in Black neighborhoods who were supporting Democrats was higher than ever before. However, a majority of Black people voted Republican and were supportive of Thompson's unsuccessful bid for reelection. Following the election, Cermak punished Black voters for their support of Thompson. His retribution included firing Black city employees from their jobs. He also increased the levels of police presence in Black communities and cracked down on illegal activities, such as gambling and prostitution, on the South Side.[4] Cermak's approach to law enforcement resulted in the arrest of an alarming number of Black residents—nearly two hundred per day (Keiser 1997: 28; see also Travis 1987). When asked about his heavy-handed approach to law enforcement in the Black community, Cermak replied that it would change when Black voters vowed to support the Democratic Party (Biles 1984: 90).

Despite his frustration with Black voters, Cermak understood that positive engagement with the Black electorate would be important if he was going to establish the Democratic Party as a dominant force in the city. Therefore, he engaged politicians Mike Sneed and Joe Tittinger, from the Second and Third Wards, to create a Black submachine for Democrats (Drake and Cayton 1962). Cermak was killed by an assassin's bullet on a trip to Miami in 1933, which left the Democratic Party without a clear leader or continued plan for engagement with the Black community.[5] Patrick Nash, Cermak's friend and the chair of the Cook County Democratic Party, seemed like the mayor's likely successor. However, Nash passed on the position, suggesting that Edward Kelly would be a better fit.

Edward Kelly also believed that the Black vote, unified

behind the Democratic Party, would increase the likelihood that the party could maintain power for the 1935 mayoral election. Although most Black Chicagoans were still Republicans at this time, Kelly kept building on Cermak's plan to bring Black voters into the Democratic Party. Upon assuming the role of mayor, he rehired individuals whom Cermak had fired from city jobs. He also appointed Black Chicagoans to higher-ranking positions in the police force, school board, and housing authority (Drake and Cayton 1962). Kelly found success in his efforts, as Black leaders demonstrated political sophistication and a willingness to choose support for their issues over attachment to their party. William Dawson and Louis B. Anderson, two Black aldermen, campaigned for Kelly in the *Chicago Defender*. In 1935, with 80 percent of the Black vote, Kelly won electoral majorities in the Second Ward and became the first Democrat to win an endorsement from the *Chicago Defender* (Biles 1984, 1995).

Once in office, Kelly continued his commitment to the Black community by sharing patronage and taking positions that were favorable to Black Chicagoans. In the lead-up to the 1943 mayoral campaign, housing became a major focus. Of frequent discussion was the proposed Hyde Park restrictive covenant, which would have excluded Black people from residency and property ownership in the all-white neighborhood. Kelly refused to sign the covenant; George McKibbin, his opponent in the primary election, did sign it. The *Chicago Defender* reported that many Black Republicans crossed party lines to vote for Kelly in the 1943 election because of his refusal to support segregated housing through the use of restrictive covenants.[6]

By 1947, Democratic Party leaders believed that Kelly had been too friendly with the Black community over the course of his administration. Democrats shut Kelly out of the party's primary nomination for mayor to support the candidacy of Martin Kennelly. Kennelly took positions that suggested that he might support Black interests. For example, in the lead-up to his primary election, he was quoted in the *Chicago Tribune* as saying, "I believe that enactment of a fair employment practices law is a practical application of the brotherhood of man principle. Accordingly, I favor the prompt enactment of a fair employment practices law."[7] Some Black leaders assumed that a vote for Kennelly would "continue and expand the progressive and far-reaching racial policies" of former mayor Kelly.[8] The *Chicago Defender* encouraged Black Chicagoans to vote for Kennelly (Hirsch 1995: 138). Despite losing in the Second Ward by 285 votes and in the Third Ward by 35 votes, Kennelly won the 1947 election.

In Kennelly, as it turned out, the Democratic Party had found a person not at all committed to pushing the Black agenda. After he took several positions on race that made him unacceptable to the Black community, it became clear that he was nothing like former mayor Kelly. Kennelly's hostile stance on racial issues cost the local Democratic Party the base of Black support that the Kelly-Nash organization had worked to build during Kelly's years as mayor. Black voters observed differences between the party at the local and presidential levels. When local Democrats deviated from the national party's increasingly liberal lead on racial issues, Black voters showed their disappointment by continuing to withhold support for the local Democratic machine while simultaneously voting for Democratic presidential candidates. In past mayoral elections, Black voters in the Second and Third Wards had supported their preferred political candidates by large margins.

As a candidate in the 1951 election, Kennelly campaigned as being "tough on crime" and chose not to meaningfully engage Black voters. When he did decide to engage with Black political leaders, it was only a few weeks before Election Day (Hirsch 2009: 140). Adding insult to injury in his relationship with the Black community, Kennelly refused to work with William L. Dawson, the city's foremost Black political leader. Black support for Democrats continued to decline, and by 1951, they were barely more competitive with Black voters than Republicans were. Black voters' evidenced their disapproval of the local Democratic Party by their limited number of votes for Democratic mayoral candidates (Grimshaw 1992: 57). In the Second Ward, Kennelly won the 1951 contest by 2,111 votes. In the Third Ward, he lost by 248 votes. In spite of a less-than-enthusiastic Black turnout, Kennelly won the 1951 mayoral contest.

Kennelly's popularity in the Black community continued to decrease over the course of his term in office. In keeping with his tough-on-crime promises, his police department was harsh on the Black community, conducting "11,562 raids that netted 24,476 individual arrests" during his administration (Hirsch 2009: 140). Also contributing to Kennelly's problems in the Black community was his feud with Dawson. The aforementioned city alderman was a well-respected figure within the Black community and would become a member of the U.S. Congress by 1955. Kennelly launched an anti-Black campaign in 1955, mostly pointed at Dawson (Hirsch 2009: 142). As a result, Black voters channeled their energy into support for a different Democratic Party nominee for the 1955 primary election.

Richard Daley, the chair of the Cook County Democrats, challenged the sitting mayor for the position in 1955. Daley had Dawson's support for his primary bid. Thanks to this backing, and in a positive reaction to the machine's decision not to slate Kennelly again, Black voters gave Daley the overwhelming majorities of their votes. Black support of Daley's mayoral campaigns extended into the 1970s and, in a few instances, made the difference in terms of his winning the reelection. For example, Black voters' importance to the Daley victory of 1963 was widely reported:[9]

> Tuesday's election saw nine predominantly Negro wards account for 77 per cent of Mayor Elect Richard J. Daley's 127,199 margin of victory. Five Central Southside wards, the 2nd, 3rd, 4th, 6th and 20th, accounted for a 49,363 edge. The 16th ward (Englewood) gave Daley a 5,840 margin and three Westside wards, the 24th, 27th and 28th, accounted for 42,473 of the bulge.[10]

Daley responded to the support from Black voters by increasing the number of Black people appointed to supervisory positions in the city council (Grimshaw 1992: 106). The Democratic machine also responded to Black voters by increasing the number of Black Chicagoans slated for office (Allswang 1977: 136). Although the spoils accorded to Black voters by Democrats were not commensurate with their levels of support, they were greater than those offered by the Republican Party.

Daley's standing among Black voters deteriorated toward the end of his career as mayor. After the 1963 victory, Daley began working to suppress the Black vote rather than mobilize it in his favor. Daley also failed to support Chicago's Black submachine. Beyond suppressing Black votes, Daley made another decision that demonstrated his intention to lessen Black political involvement. Unlike Kelly's decision to appoint Dawson as the Black submachine leader, Daley chose not to appoint a successor because doing so could threaten Daley's ability to maintain his position (Rakove 1976: 259–260). By the late 1960s, the Black population of Chicago was very large, 1.3 million among a total population of 3.3 million. Any leader of a Black political organization like Dawson's would have been well positioned to challenge Daley for the mayor's seat—and win.

Black Voters as the BOP in Elections

Part of my argument is that mayoral candidates' interactions with Black voters would have varied on the basis of fragmentation of the local political parties and the rules for election to office in a city. I expect that Chicago's politicians would have been responsive to Black voters because the city's political system included fragmented parties and single-member, residence-based political districts. This type of district made Black voters important as individuals who might shape outcomes in the city council by influencing elections in their neighborhoods even before the population was very large. As the Great Migration contributed to population growth, the political system led to the election of Black officials from Black neighborhoods.

Between 1915 and 1965, thirteen mayoral elections took place in Chicago. Black voters' potential as the BOP in these elections varied. When considering the entire Black voting age popula-

TABLE 5.2. BALANCE OF POWER POTENTIAL, CHICAGO MAYORAL ELECTIONS, 1915–1965		
Black voting age population (BVAP) estimate		
100% of BVAP	67% of BVAP	50% of BVAP
6 of 13 elections	5 of 13 elections	3 of 13 elections
Source: Compiled by the author.		

tion (BVAP), Black voters could have been the BOP in six of the thirteen elections—46 percent of the time. When considering 67 percent of the BVAP, they could have been the BOP in five elections, or 38 percent of the time. Finally, estimating 50 percent of the BVAP, Black voters could have been the BOP in three of the elections, or 23 percent of the time. At least three of the mayors—Thompson, Kennelly, and Daley—publicly acknowledged Black voters as the bloc that tipped the scale in their elections. Table 5.2 shows Black voters' BOP potential in Chicago elections from 1915 to 1965.

Another part of my argument is that politicians' beliefs about the political potential of Black voters would have shaped their behavior toward them. Further, politicians would have responded positively to Black voters in scenarios where they believed that Black voters could be the BOP in an election. I find that mayoral candidates in Chicago were responsive to Black voters. In some instances, as with Mayors Thompson, Kelly, and (in his early years) Daley, their responses were positive. These mayors campaigned for Black support and took liberal positions on race and civil rights issues. Further, they articulated their beliefs that these positions would be helpful in their attempts to earn Black votes and acknowledged Black voters as the BOP in their elections. On the other hand, Mayors Dever, Cermak, Kennelly, and Daley (in his later years) had negative responses to Black Chicagoans. They took positions that were hostile to Black interests, including ramping up law enforcement in Black communities and supporting segregated housing. These candidates ranged from thinking that the Black vote was inconsequential to working to suppress Black turnout because they believed that it was very consequential. With Kennelly's second election as the exception, the candidates for whom Black voters might be the BOP responded positively to Black voters.

Second Ward Precinct Analysis

Very little data exist about individual-level voting patterns of Black Americans before 1965. Prior to the Voting Rights Act of 1965, few localities collected information about voters' races. Therefore, to estimate voting patterns among African Americans, most scholars measure precinct-level election returns. This method is a reasonable proxy because segregation limited Black Americans to small sections of most U.S. cities. I employ this method to measure the voting activity of the Black population in Chicago's mayoral elections from 1919 to 1963.[11]

As I describe in Chapter 1, locating precinct-level data for elections during the Great Migration period is challenging. However, I was able to gain access to the precinct-level voting data for Chicago's Second Ward by working closely with the Cook County Board of Elections (BOE). The BOE maintains original, handwritten copies of election recapitulations in a warehouse near the communities under study in this book. I traveled to the warehouse to photograph the books. Later, I transcribed the ward and precinct-level data using Microsoft Excel. The rapidly changing nature of the precincts made it difficult to study changes in these areas over time. Wards changed every ten years, which also presented problems for attempting to study the period over five decades. However, because mayoral elections occurred every four years, it is possible to compare elections within the same decade. Because election districts changed frequently from 1919 to 1963, I use ward-level data rather than precinct-level data in the following analysis.

My inspection of ward data confirms the narrative put forth in this text about the political involvement of Black voters. Black voters participated in local politics as Republicans at the beginning of the period (1915 and 1919). When Mayor Thompson was unable to run in 1923, they followed his advice and voted for the

TABLE 5.3. ELECTION RECAPITULATION, CHICAGO WARD TWO, 1919–1963					
Year	Total votes	Total Democrat	Total GOP	Margin	Victor
1919	22,167	3,323	15,569	–12,246	GOP
1923	12,798	8,276	3,717	4,559	DEM
1927	27,229	1,791	24,169	–22,378	GOP
1931	20,811	3,492	16,895	–13,403	GOP
1935	26,256	20,033	5,060	14,973	DEM
1939	38,495	20,785	16,369	4,416	DEM
1943	31,067	15,637	14,533	1,104	DEM
1947	41,816	18,782	19,067	–285	GOP
1951	25,245	13,221	11,111	2,110	DEM
1955	24,139	17,856	4,440	13,416	DEM
1959	19,662	16,383	2,650	13,733	DEM
1963	19,540	15,796	2,906	12,890	DEM

Source: Chicago Board of Elections Archives, 1919–1963. Compiled by the author.
Note: A negative number indicates a win for the Republican candidates.

Democratic candidate. Their support returned to the Republican Party for 1927 and 1931. They began supporting Democrats in 1935 and continued through the period under study here. The only exception was the 1947 mayoral election, when many of them broke ranks with Democrats to vote against Kennelly. That year, Democrats lost the Second Ward by 285 votes and the Third Ward by 35 votes.

The 1923 and 1947 election contests are important to examine because they demonstrate the political sophistication of Chicago's Black electorate. These elections also demonstrate the potential impact that candidates' positions on racial issues might have had on Black electoral participation. In 1923, Black Chicagoans crossed party lines to vote strategically and support their "friend," Mayor Thompson. In 1947, they voted against a mayor with racist policies and a racist campaign. Table 5.3 shows the election results, discussed above, of Chicago's Second Ward from 1919 to 1963.

Black Political Office Holders

Conditions were right for Black people in Illinois to be elected to legislative positions relatively early in the Great Migration period. Although the size of the Black population was a tiny percentage of the city's population at the beginning of the era, the sheer number of Black people in Chicago was second only to that of New York's Black population. The total number of Black people living in Chicago and their percentage of the total voting age population (TVAP) grew exponentially between 1915 and 1965. Adding to Black Chicagoans' electoral success was a system of housing segregation and cumulative voting for positions in the Illinois state legislature (Gosnell 1967: 56). Fifty-three Black Chicagoans held elected positions in the state legislature, city council, and U.S. Congress from 1915 to 1965; twenty-nine of them, or 54.7 percent, were migrants.

The system of voting at the local level was straightforward. For most of the period, members of the city council were elected from single-member, residence-based districts. Elections to the state legislature were different, with each senatorial district sending three individuals to the state house of representatives. Black voters in Chicago often strategically reserved their three votes for members of their race. This practice allowed them to win elected office in the state legislature even before the Black population grew very large through the Great Migration. The following section describes Black Chicagoans' work generally in the state legislature, city council, and U.S. Congress. Then, I look at Black elected officials' work in the city council. Finally, I consider the work of Chicago's three Black members of the U.S. Congress before providing concluding comments about the city.

Among the cities under consideration in this book, Chicago leads Detroit and New York in the total number of Black people holding political office during the Great Migration era. However, formal political participation differed for Black elected officials in Chicago. Political machines played a much larger role in their legislative lives and often led them to moderate their

Figure 5.1. State representative and migrant Floy Clements at a political dinner, August 1960. (Walter Sanders/The LIFE Picture Collection/Getty Images.)

positions on racial issues or fail to meaningfully consider them at all. In a number of instances, Black lawmakers refused to take positions that differed from the wishes of political bosses in the city. Political positioning by bosses also hindered Black lawmakers' ability to pass legislation in a few instances.

Chicago also had the worst record of electing Black women to office among the cities in this book. Between 1915 and 1965, just one Black woman held a position in the state legislature or city council; by comparison, New York had three and Detroit had five. Floy Clements, pictured in Figure 5.1, was a migrant from Memphis, Tennessee, and the first Black woman to represent Chicago in the state legislature. In 1958, she was elected to the Illinois House of Representatives. During her campaign, she expressed interest in civil rights issues, including access to education, construction of schools, and efforts to establish a Fair Employment Practices Committee (FEPC).[12] Clements served one term in the state legislature. Nearly twenty years later, in

1976, Earlean Collins would become the first Black woman to be elected to the Illinois State Senate. No woman served on Chicago's city council until after the Great Migration period. Anna Langford, a Black woman who came to Chicago from Ohio, would become the first Black woman elected to the Chicago City Council in 1971 and serve three nonconsecutive terms.[13] Chicago's failure to elect Black women is curious, given that the city had larger numbers of Black people in elected office than New York and Detroit. However, considering the strong role of the political machines in determining who would be nominated for office and the exclusion of women from party leadership, the lack of elected women in Chicago is unsurprising.

Black Chicagoans in the State Legislature

Black Chicagoans started getting elected to the state legislature relatively early, compared to Black voters in Detroit and New York, winning competitive elections in the 1870s and 1880s. The number of Black people in the state legislature fluctuated from 1915 to 1965. In 1916, the legislature included two Black elected officials. That number increased to three from 1918 to 1922 and oscillated between five and six from 1924 to 1952. In 1954, the legislature included seven Black elected officials. Following a 1956 redistricting in the state, that number increased to ten.[14]

In 1876, John W. E. Thomas became the first Black person elected to the state legislature in Illinois, and a Black person has continuously been elected to the Illinois state legislature since 1882. In 1924, Adelbert Roberts became the highest-ranking Black American in any state legislature when he ran for and won a seat in the Illinois State Senate. By the time of Roberts's election, the Third District was so overwhelmingly Black and Republican that Democratic Party leaders decided not expend resources to contest the election. Roberts ran unopposed for the seat.[15] Between 1924 and 1965, the state senate included at least one Black person. Of the thirty-eight Black people who served in the Illinois state legislature from 1915 to 1965, twenty-one of them, or 55 percent, were migrants.

General Legislative Concerns of Black Officials in the State Legislature

Black members of the Illinois legislature had the same political concerns as their counterparts in Michigan and New York: they were primarily worried about issues of discrimination in various parts of their lives. Housing was a major focus, as was discrimination in jobs and education.

The Great Migration exacerbated Chicago's existing housing problem. As the Black population grew, it had fewer places to live because of segregation within the city. Black members of the state legislature were cognizant of these problems, and some of them sought to pass legislation that would protect Black people from poor housing conditions and discrimination. Owners and landlords frequently modified dwellings so they could accommodate larger numbers of people than they should have safely housed. These housing violations became increasingly problematic, as many buildings in the Southside experienced fires and other problems because of overpopulation. To combat these problems, as the state legislature was trying to regulate the redevelopment activities of corporations in 1941, State Representative Charles Jenkins—a migrant from Texas—suggested an amendment to the legislation that would require corporations to accept rental applications from all people, regardless of their race.[16]

A related housing issue was slum clearance and redevelopment. Developers sought to seize land in Black communities through eminent domain, arguing that their real estate investments would add value to the city. Black Chicagoans worried that the actual impact would include displacing and dismantling their communities. In 1939, a group of Black state legislators worked to prevent an eminent domain bill that would have allowed the construction of privately developed, expensive, high-rise housing in places where many of their Black constituents lived. Jenkins invoked the filibuster as a method of stopping the legislation from moving forward. Representative Ernest A. Greene—originally from Georgia—followed up by introducing an amendment that would gut the bill of its most harmful parts.[17] The eminent domain battle continued into the next legislative session, as

State Senator William A. Wallace—originally from Maryland—worked on a number of housing issues. He tried unsuccessfully to prevent the passage of slum clearance legislation in 1941 by suggesting several amendments to the bill,[18] but in the end, special interests were able to overcome his objections.

Later in the period, Cecil Partee—a migrant from Arkansas—tried unsuccessfully to legislate open housing in Illinois. In 1963, he sponsored legislation to prohibit discrimination in the sale and rental of certain housing units. The legislation initially received support from the Daley machine, but ultimately, Daley signaled that Democrats were not required to support the bill. In the absence of pressure from the Democratic machine, many lawmakers declined to vote for the anti-discrimination bill.[19] This kind of situation was common because the demands of party leaders served as a guidepost for many elected officials' positions on issues.

People left the South with hopes of finding work. However, many Black newcomers to Chicago confronted systems that conspired to shut them out of the labor market by giving preference to every other racial/ethnic group (Kersten 1998). Black members of the Illinois state legislature worked to pass laws that would prevent employment discrimination. For example, State Representatives Charles Jenkins and William Warfield successfully passed HB 621 in 1941.[20] This legislation created financial penalties for defense contractors who discriminated against laborers on the basis of race. For many years, Black members of the Illinois state legislature also worked to establish an FEPC in the state. Greene introduced the state's first attempt at an FEPC law. The bill passed in the state assembly but failed in the senate. Year after year, the measure passed in the assembly before dying for lack of support in the senate. In the later part of the period, Mississippi migrant and State Assemblyman Corneal Davis continued the effort to establish an FEPC in the state. With support from the governor, Davis's legislation finally passed in 1961. Governor Otto Kerner later won his gubernatorial reelection using support for the FEPC as a prominent part of his campaign.[21]

The practice of job discrimination existed in the public as well as private sectors. In 1961, State Senator Fred Smith—a migrant from Texas—learned that employees in the Department of Labor and in the Illinois Free Employment Service were using a coding system to separate Black applicants from the total pool of applicants. Smith remarked, "It is ironical . . . that on one hand, Negroes are criticized for having to resort to public relief, and then on the other hand a state agency would use a code to deny the same people an opportunity of legitimate employment." In response, Smith introduced legislation that would criminalize intentional discrimination by agency employees.[22]

Education was another concern for members of the Illinois state legislature. Problems with access to education for residents of Chicago manifested in a number of ways over the migration period. Many schools sought to exclude Black people from admission. Early in the period, this discrimination was especially true for Black students seeking to enroll in cosmetology, business, and vocational classes. In response, State Assemblyman Charles Griffin sponsored a bill that would put these institutions' standing in jeopardy for discriminating against Black students.[23] His bill, which also stipulated that graduates of schools with discriminatory practices would be barred from taking state licensing exams, passed the state house of representatives. With assistance from Senator Adolph Marks, a white ally, the bill passed the senate and became law.[24]

Later in the period, Black state legislators asserted that Chicago schools were segregated in ways that were illegal and unnecessary. State Representative Charles Armstrong—a migrant from North Carolina—alleged that segregated classrooms in white neighborhoods were sitting empty while Black schools on the South Side had to work in double shifts to educate students. In 1959, with the support of the eight other Black state representatives, Armstrong introduced legislation that would prevent school boards from drawing district lines that promoted segregation.[25] "It is to stop boards of education from hiding behind the curtain of residential segregation in promoting segregation in the public schools," Armstrong told reporters.[26] The legislation had mixed results. In some instances, school lines were redrawn; in others, districts exploited loopholes in the law to protect segregation. For example, rather than let Black students enter school buildings, some school officials created mobile classrooms to house Black children during the day.[27] Black members of the state legislature and the city council worked together to try to convince Mayor Daley to take action to solve the problem.

Beyond the issues of anti-discrimination in housing, jobs, and education, members of the state legislature in Illinois had other concerns related to racial violence and discrimination. When Illinois experienced a rise in activity of the Ku Klux Klan (KKK) in the early part of the Great Migration, Black members of the state legislature responded. Illinois's first Black state senator, Roberts, introduced legislation that would fine individuals who were found masked or hooded when detained for disturbing the peace.[28] Louisiana migrant and State Senator William King worked on a number of anti-KKK measures, including bills that would require members of private organizations, such as the KKK, to provide lists of their members. He also led an effort to encourage the Illinois state legislature to compel the U.S. Congress to pass anti-lynching legislation.[29] Following a 1946 lynching in Monroe, Georgia, Representative Charles Skyles—who came to Chicago from Arkansas—got the state assembly to adopt a resolution condemning the event.[30]

Black Chicagoans in Local Elected Positions

Unlike in New York, a seat on the city council was considered an important position for Black elected officials in Chicago. Although they had been able to win seats in the state legislature by the late 1880s, Black Chicagoans were not elected to the city council until the 1915 election of De Priest. By 1959, six Black men were serving on the city council.[31] They also began to have access to powerful committees within the city council. For example, Kenneth Campbell was appointed to the Committee on Committees and Rules in 1959. Black elected officials in the city council had many of the same legislative concerns as their counterparts in the state legislature. For example, fair housing, as well as access to education and employment, received attention from Black city council members. However, once the Democratic Party became dominant in the city, Black city council members were seemingly more concerned about maintaining the official position of their political party than challenging the party to advocate for their issues. During the 1960s, six Black aldermen were so unwilling to act outside the wishes of Mayor Daley and the political machine that they became known as the "silent six." Later, they would disagree among themselves about the best approach to politics as the numbers of those inclined to challenge the party grew in the 1960s.

In 1961, for example, Black members of the city council were divided regarding legislation that would reform police practices in the city. The superintendent of police and the police force were split on the legislation, with most of the rank-and-file police officers disagreeing with city leadership. Mayor Daley made it clear that he agreed with the superintendent's belief that reforms were needed. When it came time for the city council to decide on the measure, Black council members were on opposite sides: William Harvey and Robert Miller sided with the police, while Claude Holman supported the mayor. Ralph Metcalfe, Kenneth Campbell, and Benjamin Lewis did not take a position.[32]

When the problem of segregated schools came to a head in Chicago, Black city council members were less vocal about civil rights issues and more conservative than their counterparts in the state legislature, although a few of them were willing to agitate for progress on the issue. Black members of the city council frequently mentioned that they did not support the work of such groups as the Student Nonviolent Coordinating Committee (SNCC) and the Congress of Racial Equality (CORE) that came to the city to fight for progress, remarking that they "d[idn't] like their tactics."[33]

Legislative Concerns of Black Migrants in the City Council

As described above, many problems with housing in Chicago stemmed from a lack of available and affordable units as well as systems that were designed to facilitate segregation. The problems with discrimination in housing evolved between 1915 and 1965, as did the ways in which white residents went about enforcing segregation. In 1948, seeking to limit these practices, Aldermen Archibald Carey and William H. Harvey introduced an ordinance that would end discrimination in public housing.[34] The bill proposed that publicly funded housing should not be segregated. Further, it proposed that slum clearance and redevelopment in the city should occur in a manner that would not disproportionately affect residents on the basis of their race or religion. This legislation also stipulated that current residents must have a say in changes that might occur in their communities. The Black aldermen were joined in support for the legislation by Alderman Abraham Cohen of the Fourth Ward.

Open access to housing was still a concern in the later part of the period. In the 1960s, aldermen tried various methods to improve housing conditions in the city. In 1960, Claude Holman and Leon Despres, a white, liberal alderman from the Fifth Ward, attempted to pass legislation for open housing in the city.[35] They went further, arguing that the city should pass legislation that would apply to the entire state. Republicans sought to block the measure by arguing that the city government did not have jurisdiction to prevent discrimination across the state. In an attempt to move the legislation along and speak directly to conservatives' criticisms, Holman asked the city lawyer to determine the city's jurisdiction and the validity of the Republicans' claims. City lawyers eventually sided with Republicans and deemed the 1961 version of the open housing bill unconstitutional.[36]

Holman sponsored a different version of the anti-discrimination legislation, which passed in September 1963. The ordinance banned discrimination by real estate brokers in the sale or rental of housing in the city.[37] One of the factors contributing to the passage of the 1963 ordinance was pressure from Mayor Daley on Democratic members of the city council to change their votes.[38] Daley's involvement with this vote was noteworthy because of its timing. Daley was fresh off his 1959 reelection, which he won by a comfortable margin without supporting Holman's proposal for open housing. In 1963, however, he was up for reelection in a close contest against Benjamin Adamowski. Daley's 1963 election was one of the few in Chicago in which Black voters could have been the BOP, with 50 percent participation of the BVAP.

Economic opportunity was part of the promise of the Great Migration and Chicago. However, many migrants found that they could not fully participate in the labor market. Employers in various sectors discriminated against Black job seekers. In 1945, Aldermen William Harvey and Oscar De Priest worked with the Chicago Civil Liberties Committee to introduce fair employment laws in the city council.[39] The measure passed, making Chicago the first city in the nation to enact legislation banning employment discrimination.

Black elected officials also made efforts to correct for discrimination in city contracts with outside entities. Public utility companies had a long-standing practice of discriminating against Black workers. When the city decided to build public transportation, it did so through a private utilities firm that continued the practice of discrimination. The city's Black leaders responded in two ways. Some members of the city council worked with community organizations to demand hiring quotas for Black residents.[40] Earl B. Dickerson—a migrant from Mississippi—used his position as alderman to agitate against discrimination in hiring. With support from Chicago native and alderman Benjamin Grant, Dickerson proposed bringing the construction of public rail under city control. Under an amendment to the Unified Traction Ordinance, the hiring practices of private utility companies would be wholly subject to the government's anti-discrimination rules.[41] The law would open new avenues of employment as train operators, bus drivers, and other fields in transportation that had been closed to Black Chicagoans. Dickerson fought opponents for two years on the measure. Ultimately, he was successful in getting the city council to support the ordinance, and the measure passed after being approved by voters (Blakely and Shepard 2006: 80–81).

The Great Migration in the Illinois State Legislature

Chicago's migrant elected officials' political priorities were not markedly different from those of their northern-born counterparts. In some instances, they did mention their own migrations in their descriptions of policy positions. Metcalfe—whose migration from Georgia is described in this book's Introduction—expressed concern about education standards in Chicago as he told the *Chicago Defender*, "My mother and father left Atlanta when I was seven so that we could get a better education."[42] In some instances, the migrants also used the example of the South to shame their counterparts into support for their positions. For example, when members of the Illinois state legislature wrote a bill to prevent assistance to "illiterate voters," Black State Senator Smith—a migrant from Texas—told his colleagues:

> You dare not substitute the philosophy of Abraham Lincoln with that of Strom Thurmond of the Carolinas. You seek here to follow reasoning of Governor Wallace of Alabama against whom Dr. Martin Luther King has waged such a determined fight. Illinois would be taking a backward step were your sort of reasoning to prevail, and I am sure that the House of Representatives which has, during this session, displayed a more reasonable and just attitude than has this senate will most certainly defeat this legislation.[43]

One of the legislative areas of specific concern to Chicago migrants in the electorate was "relief," or welfare. Although most migrants came to Chicago on the promise of jobs and prosperity, not everyone found success when they arrived. In some instances, migrants found jobs upon arrival but then lost them or underestimated the cost of maintaining a family in the city. The result was that some of the newcomers to the city, Black and white, ended up seeking assistance from the government to make ends meet.

White residents of Illinois commonly argued that the southern migrants cost state taxpayers too much. Further, they claimed that Black migrants to Chicago got more than they deserved from the state government because they were not paying into the system. In response, and as a result of problems with the state welfare agency and budget, Illinois lawmakers established policies stipulating that families had to live in Chicago for at least one year before they were eligible for welfare. The limitations on and cuts to the state welfare program were a source of animus for Black lawmakers, who had to manage requests from newly arrived residents needing assistance before the one-year mark. In 1962, this concern was also reflected in the city council. After the state expressed a need to cut relief to families by 10 percent, the six Black members of the Chicago City Council introduced a resolution asking the governor not to cut relief funding.[44] Governor Otto Kerner initially protested but changed his position to remove the cut from his budget after Mayor Daley stepped in to echo the Black members' sentiments.[45]

Congress

All three members of the U.S. Congress from Chicago were migrants: Oscar S. De Priest (1929–1935), Arthur Mitchell (1935–1943), and William Dawson (1943–1970). De Priest experienced two notable firsts in his political career: he was the first Black person elected to the city council in Chicago, and he was the first Black person elected to Congress after Reconstruction.[46] As a member of Congress, De Priest worked on a number of Black issues. As a newcomer to Congress, and the first Black person to return to office in the twenty-eight years since the end of Reconstruction, De Priest faced problems of segregation and discrimination in the Capitol and among some of his colleagues.

As the only Black person in Congress at the time, De Priest considered issues that were important to Black voters across the nation in addition to those affecting his Chicago constituents. In many instances, his measures lacked the support from his colleagues they needed to pass. Some of the unsuccessful bills he introduced included anti-lynching measures for state and local governments and legislation that would allow courts to relocate trials if defendants might not have access to fair proceedings because of their race. In spite of these challenges, De Priest did experience some success, such as the addition of an anti-discrimination clause to a 1933 relief bill.

Mitchell and Dawson were more passive in their approach to legislation that addressed concerns of Black people throughout the nation. Mitchell introduced and supported legislation that would end discrimination in the military and in government hiring. However, he drew criticism from the National Association for the Advancement of Colored People (NAACP) in 1935 when he introduced anti-lynching legislation that was less punitive than a bill that this organization had already proposed. In the process of antagonizing the NAACP, Mitchell believed that he had made friends with racial conservatives. However, when it came time to support Mitchell's legislation, southern Democrats and other Republicans voted against him and caused his bill to fail. Eventually, the NAACP's version of the bill passed, after a brutal murder in Mississippi caused renewed conversation on the topic (Nordin 1997).

Like Mitchell, Dawson began his political career prioritizing issues other than race and civil rights. However, these issues were not absent. Of note was his work to ensure that the military remained desegregated following the 1948 executive order by President Harry Truman. He also opposed poll tax legislation under the belief that it would be especially unfair to Black and low-income Americans. In 1963, Dawson introduced legislation on civil rights that would eventually become part of the 1964 Civil Rights Act. However, leaders and laypersons in the Black community criticized Dawson for his passive approach to Black issues. Many suggested that he had greater loyalty to the Democratic Party and to his own political aspirations than to his race.[47]

Conclusion

The party system in Chicago was very strong, which influenced mayoral candidates, Black voters, and Black elected officials in different ways. The strength of the party machines often made primary elections the most important in the cycle. Therefore, mayoral candidates were calculating in their attempts to manage Black voters. Most of the mayoral candidates attended to the Black community in positive ways, taking positions that might garner Black support and sharing limited amounts of patronage with the community during their mayoral administrations. In a couple of cases, mayoral candidates' posture toward Black voters negatively changed once they were elected to office. Some of the mayoral candidates' interactions were completely negative. They refused to campaign for Black votes, arguing that they did not need or want Black support. These candidates also took positions that were hostile to the Black community as a way to earn greater support among white communities.

Black voters exercised their power by voting for individuals who they believed would advocate for their interests. Their strategic behavior contributed to the victories of Dever and Daley. They also used voting rules to elect Black people to the state legislature relatively early in the Great Migration period. Black Chicagoans won elections to political office earlier than did their counterparts in New York and Detroit. However, many of them were constrained by the requirements of a large and strong party organization. Although they had improvement of Black life and anti-discrimination legislation as their focus, many of them were passive in their approach to these issues. The number of Black elected officials who were willing to buck the party grew after the Great Migration period, once the party machine lost its strength and other civil rights organizations came to the city to fight for progress in housing and education.

Conclusion

Many of the great advances in Black politics occurred as the Great Migration was ending in the 1960s. While Black people were still migrating to cities in the North in the late 1950s and 1960s, white residents were deserting urban areas in favor of the suburbs. As a result, Black people began to constitute even larger percentages of the population in Chicago, Detroit, and other major cities. As time passed and these populations grew, Black people continued winning elections to positions in state legislatures and city councils. For example, J. Raymond Jones became the first Black leader of New York's Tammany Hall in 1964. A few years later, in 1967, Carl Stokes won his campaign to become the mayor of Cleveland, making him the first Black mayor of a major U.S. city. The cities under study in this book would elect their own Black mayors in the following decades: Coleman Young became the mayor of Detroit in 1974, Harold Washington was elected the mayor of Chicago in 1983, and David Dinkins won the mayor's seat in New York in 1990. None of these electoral victories could have been achieved without the Great Migration.

Mayoral Interactions

Millions of Black Americans left the South, hoping to make better lives for themselves, and changed American politics through their movement. In Detroit, New York, and Chicago, candidates for political office took note of the demographic changes caused by the Great Migration. White politicians often believed that Black voters had political power and that their increased numbers in northern cities might make them the balance of power (BOP) in elections. Therefore, they strategized to manage the increasing number of Black voters in the electorate.

Politicians' responses varied according to their political environments. Detroit's city charter called for nonpartisan, at-large city elections. Most mayoral candidates in Detroit responded negatively to Black voters. They worked to unify and mobilize the white electorate against any attempt—by members of the Black community, union organizations, or white liberal political candidates—to provide equal access to jobs or housing in the city. New York had a strong party machine as well as many smaller party organizations and third parties. Therefore, politicians' response to Black voters was more frequently positive. New York politicians understood that Black voters could be an important part of any broad coalition for the votes necessary to win a mayoral election. Chicago also had a strong party machine, although it was dominated by just one party. Mayoral candidates' responses were split, with candidates' interest in Black voters varying based on competition in the party.

Many politicians and political observers of the time described Black voters as the BOP in elections. Building on previous works about Black voters as the BOP, I seek to determine whether this perception of Black voting strength is plausible for the fifty mayoral elections that took place in Detroit, New York, and Chicago from 1915 to 1965. Assuming 100 percent of the Black voting age population (BVAP), Black voters might have been the BOP in thirty-one of the mayoral elections, or 62 percent of the time. When I consider 67 percent of the BVAP, Black voters might have been the BOP in twenty-two elections, or 44 percent of the time. In my most conservative estimates, assuming 50 percent turnout of the BVAP, Black voters could have been the BOP in seventeen elections, or 34 percent of the time.

As I use the term *balance of power*, building on Henry Lee Moon's 1948 calculation and book by the same name, Black voters were not the BOP in most of the mayoral elections under study here—if one considers the highest threshold for turnout. However, politicians' attention to and concern with Black voters was reasonable, given their growth in the northern electorates. Although Black voters did not always have the ability to change the outcome of an election as a single group, they did contribute to coalitions of voters as large blocs of individuals who were willing to vote strategically for their interests. Future work should revise the BOP concept as it is used to describe Black voters during this time to account for their place among many groups in the electorate.

Black Elected Officials

Black people were able to leverage the power of Black voters to win election to political offices themselves. From 1915 to 1965, 121 of them won elections to legislative positions in city government, state legislatures, and the U.S. Congress. Seventy of the Black elected officials in Detroit, New York, and Chicago were participants in the Great Migration. In other words, more than half—57 percent—of the Black elected office holders were participants in the Great Migration. These migrants' stories varied, with some of them choosing to come to the North through their own volition and many others of them coming as children. Regardless of how they got to the North, it is remarkable that so many of these individuals were able to build political careers so soon after establishing new homes.

As legislators, Black elected officials were most often concerned with policies that would improve the lives of members of their race. I find it disheartening that many of the legislative priorities of Black elected officials from 1915 to 1965 are similar to the concerns of today. Black elected officials of the

Great Migration era were interested in anti-discrimination measures related to public accommodations, jobs, and housing. They were also worried about law enforcement in their communities. Migrants, as elected officials, did not have legislative priorities that differed very much from those of their northern-born counterparts. However, in a few instances, they did demonstrate concern for issues that were specific to migrants. In particular, some migrant elected officials sought legislation to protect agricultural workers during harvest seasons.

The American politics literature has come a long way in reframing our understandings of changes in the major political parties over the course of the twentieth century. These revisions provide new ways to think about what was happening with white political actors. They also describe the actions of interest groups and political parties. However, one of the through lines in the literature is an absence of people. Scholars often read and think about developments in civil rights in terms of entire legislatures and political parties or interest groups, with blocs of actors on various sides of the issues. More to the point, with regard to work on civil rights, Black people are frequently absent from our writings about twentieth-century party development.

One of the points this book demonstrates is that Black people were present and active in the body politic. They were voters and members of interest groups as well as political elites. Further, many of the developments in civil rights were marked with the fingerprints of Black elected officials. If you look closely at what happened with individual pieces of racially liberal northern legislation, you will often find that Black elected officials—many of them migrants—were at the genesis of this work. In many instances, Black elected officials introduced the initial versions of bills that went on to become landmark legislation. I hope this book highlights some of the individuals who changed politics in the North through their Great Migration and through their service to their communities.

Although the Great Migration has not been the focus of stories of national party development, scholars have been uncovering and beginning to point to its import for the larger story of party change in America (see Schickler 2016). Black people who were leaving the South for the North went to places where they thought they could find work and be free from discrimination. In many instances, that decision meant that they settled in the largest cities of the largest states in the country. This relocation made them an important factor in the Electoral College (EC) strategy. National politicians were thoughtful about ways in which they could engage Black voters to their benefit. They also believed that Black voters had political power and explicitly described them as the BOP in some presidential elections.

I choose to highlight the stories of three cities, with diverse political systems, whose populations grew because of the Great Migration. Detroit, New York, and Chicago are important as three of the cities with the largest numbers of Black people outside the South. However, other cities warrant detailed consideration. Particularly interesting might be works on the political development of medium-sized northern cities, places in the Border South, or northern cities where Black populations constituted a greater percentage of the overall population. The political impact of migration to the West is also worthy of study. Although most Black people moved west during the second wave of the Great Migration, their presence was consequential for state and local governments in that region. A more detailed comparison of participants in the Great Migration to Caribbean immigrants presents another opportunity for research. Christina Greer's (2013) work describes the current political participation of Black ethnic groups in New York City. However, we can learn more about the political participation of Black immigrants to America during earlier periods.

The story of Black women deserves attention. Black women were 9 of the 121 Black elected officials in these three cities from 1915 to 1965. The small number of Black women in elected office in Chicago is curious given the city's large number of Black elected officials. It seems intuitive that a larger number of Black elected officials in a city would increase the likelihood that Black women might have been elected to office. However, it was extremely difficult to get elected to office from outside the party apparatus in Chicago, and the parties did not nominate many Black women for political offices. Therefore, Chicago, with the largest number of Black people elected to office, had the smallest number of Black women in elected positions—just one. By contrast, Detroit had the largest number of Black women in elected office—five. New York, with the second-largest population of Black elected officials, also had the second-largest Black woman delegation—three.

I chose to focus on legislative positions because they were consistent across the jurisdictions. However, Black people struggled to gain access to a variety of government positions during the period of interest. Gaining access to judgeships was a top concern of Black people in these cities. Beyond the elected positions, there is also much more to learn about how such Black political titans as Edward H. Wright and J. Raymond Jones worked behind the scenes in the parties to shape Black political outcomes. There is also space to learn about Black peoples' ascendance to appointed positions. Some of this work is done in Hanes Walton's *Black Politics* (1972) and Harold Foote Gosnell's *Negro Politicians* (1967). However, many developments have occurred since the publication of these works.

Current Considerations in Black Migration

Many Black people are moving away from the places where the Great Migration took them or their ancestors in a few new forms of migration. Beginning in the 1970s, southern migration to the North began to reverse. A Return Migration is underway, as many young Black people flock to the urban South in search of the same things their ancestors sought: jobs and opportunity. Such cities as Atlanta, Charlotte, and Houston now top the lists of places where young Black people say they would like to settle. Similarly, some Black senior citizens have migrated to areas in the South where they are able to retire comfortably because of the lower cost of living. This influx of upwardly mobile Black residents has had and will continue to have important consequences for state and local politics throughout the South.

In 2018, two young Black politicians ran groundbreaking campaigns for governor in Georgia and Florida. Stacey Abrams—a Black woman—ran as the first Black person and female Democratic gubernatorial nominee of Georgia. Andrew Gillum—a Black man—ran as the first Black Democratic Party nominee for governor of the state of Florida. In both instances, the demographic changes that have occurred in the period since the Great Migration have changed the course of politics. Florida is an especially interesting case because its growth has been rapid and steady. Whereas it was only the ninth-largest state in 1970, it is the third-largest state as of 2019. This growth coupled with increasing racial and ideological diversity among its new residents made it possible for Gillum to come within a fraction of a point of the state's highest elected position.

These demographic changes—and, by extension, changes to the electorate—also influence local politics. The elections following the 2016 cycle included many notable Black electoral victories. In 2017, for example, there was remarkable growth in the number of Black mayors serving their cities for the first time, including Brendon Barber in Georgetown, South Carolina; Booker Gainor in Cairo, Georgia; Vi Lyles in Charlotte, North Carolina; Jonathan McCollar in Statesboro, Georgia; Craig Newton in Gwinnett, Atlanta; Mary Parham-Copelan in Milledgeville, Georgia; and Frank Scott in Little Rock, Arkansas.[1]

Another trend in the current Black migration is the movement of Black populations out of major cities into inner-ring suburbs as gentrification and redevelopment lead to the displacement of long-time city residents. Gentrification has political consequences for the cities that Black populations leave as well as the places where they settle. As Black residents leave major cities, they take with them the ability to sustain the strong, Black political voice that came into existence as a result of the Great Migration. This situation may be especially true for positions that require citywide support to win elected office.

One example of this shift could be observed in the 2016 race for mayor of Atlanta. Many people describe Atlanta as the epicenter of the "new" South and Black achievement, so it should follow that electing Black officials to a citywide office would be simple. However, many of the Black people living in the Atlanta area actually live outside the city limits. Therefore, Keisha Lance Bottoms faced a highly competitive race for mayor against a white female opponent in 2016.[2] Bottoms eventually won the election by 832 votes. The Atlanta mayoral race presents questions about the future of Black politicians who once would have been able to win their positions easily just by running in cities with large Black populations. As of this writing, many Black residents of Washington, D.C., have questions about whether Muriel Bowser, the current Black mayor of the former "Chocolate City"—now "Latte City"—will be its last.

Appendix

TABLE A.1. BLACK ELECTED OFFICIALS, DETROIT			
Name	**Migrant?**	**Birthplace**	**Political office(s)**
Bradley, James	Yes	Hope, Arkansas	State senator
Brown, Basil W.	No	Vandalia, Michigan	State senator
*Brown, Cora	Yes	Bessemer, Alabama	State senator
Brown, Joseph	Yes	Knoxville, Tennessee	State senator
Bryant, Bristoe	Yes	Huntingdon, Tennessee	State senator
Cartwright, Arthur	Yes	Madison County, Alabama	State representative
Conyers, John, Jr.	No	Detroit, Michigan	Congressman
Currie, Edgar	Yes	Newport, Arkansas	State representative
Del Rio, James	No	Detroit, Michigan	State representative
Diggs, Charles C., Jr.	No	Detroit, Michigan	Congressman
Diggs, Charles C., Sr.	Yes	Tallula, Mississippi	State senator
Diggs, Charles M.	Yes	Winston-Salem, North Carolina	State representative
Diggs, O. Roosevelt	No	Detroit, Michigan	State representative
Edwards, George H.	Yes	Brunswick, Georgia	State representative
*Elliott, Daisy	No	Filbert, West Virginia	State representative
*Ferguson, Rosetta A.	Yes	Florence, Mississippi	State representative
Holmes, David S., Jr.	Yes	Covington, Kentucky	State representative
Hood, Nicholas	No	Terre Haute, Indiana	City council member
Hood, Raymond W.	No	Detroit, Michigan	State representative
McNeely, Matthew	Yes	Millen, Georgia	State representative
Patrick, William	Yes	Washington, DC	City council member
Roxborough, Charles A., III	Yes	Plaquemine, Louisiana	State senator
West, Daniel	Yes	Algood, Tennessee	State representative
*White, Charline	Yes	Atlanta, Georgia	State representative
White, Horace	Yes	Cave Spring, Georgia	State representative
Yates, Frederick	Yes	Malvern, Arkansas	State representative
Young, Coleman A.	Yes	Tuscaloosa, Alabama	State senator/mayor
*Young, Maxcine	Yes	Laurens, South Carolina	State representative

Source: Compiled by the author.
Note: 28 Black elected officials, 20 migrants.
*Denotes a woman in office.

TABLE A.2. BLACK ELECTED OFFICIALS, NEW YORK			
Name	**Migrant?**	**Birthplace**	**Political office(s)**
Andrews, William T.	Yes	Sumter, South Carolina	State assemblyman
Archibald, Julius A.	No	Trinidad, British West Indies	State senator
Baker, Bertram	No	Nevis, British West Indies	State assemblyman
Billups, Pope B.	Yes	Athens, Georgia	State assemblyman
Brown, Earl	Yes	Charlottesville, Virginia	City council member
Browne, Kenneth N.	No	New York, New York	State assemblyman
*Buchanan, Bessie A.	No	New York, New York	State assemblywoman
Burrows, Daniel L.	Yes	Cape Charles, Virginia	State assemblyman
*Chisholm, Shirley	No	New York, New York	State assemblywoman
Crump, Elijah L.	Yes	Washington, DC	State assemblyman
Davis, Benjamin J., Jr.	Yes	Dawson, Georgia	City council member
Dickens, Lloyd E.	Yes	Tulsa, Oklahoma	State assemblyman
Dickens, Thomas	Yes	Tulsa, Oklahoma	State assemblyman
Diggs, J. Daniel	Yes	Sumter, North Carolina	Alderman
Evans, Herbert B.	No	Kansas City, Missouri	City council member
Gladwin, Walter H.	No	Verbice, British Guiana	State assemblyman
Harris, George W.	No	Topeka, Kansas	Alderman
Hawkins, John Clifford	Yes	Middleburg, North Carolina	Alderman/state assemblyman
Jack, Hulan	No	Windwards, St. Lucia	State assemblyman
Johnson, Conrad A.	No	Barbados, British West Indies	Alderman
Johnson, Edward Austin	Yes	Raleigh, North Carolina	State assemblyman
Jones, J. Raymond	No	Charlotte Amalie, Dutch West Indies	City council member

Name	Migrant?	Birthplace	Political office(s)
Jones, Thomas R.	No	New York, New York	State assemblyman
Justice, Robert W.	Yes	Charlotte, North Carolina	State assemblyman
Moore, Fred R.	Yes	Washington, DC	Alderman
*Motley, Constance Baker	No	New Haven, Connecticut	State assemblywoman
Perkins, Lamar	Yes	Savannah, Georgia	State assemblyman
Pinckney, Joseph	Yes	Frogmore, South Carolina	State assemblyman
Powell, Adam Clayton	No	New York, New York	City council member/ congressman
Rivers, Francis E.	Yes	Kansas City, Kansas	State assemblyman
Roberts, Charles H.	Yes	North Carolina	Alderman
Shields, Henri W.	Yes	Knoxville, Tennessee	State assemblyman/ alderman
Smith, John W.	Yes	Petersburg, Virginia	Alderman
Stephens, James E.	No	Steelton, Pennsylvania	State assemblyman
Stevens, Harold E.	Yes	Johns Island, South Carolina	State assemblyman
Thomas, James C.	No	New York, New York	State assemblyman
Thompson, William C.	No	New York, New York	City council member/state senator
Turner, Leslie T.	Yes	Waverly, Virginia	State assemblyman
Warner, Ivan	No	New York, New York	State assemblyman
Watson, James L.	No	New York, New York	State senator

Source: Compiled by the author.
Note: 40 Black elected officials, 21 migrants.
*Denotes a woman in office.

TABLE A.3. BLACK ELECTED OFFICIALS, CHICAGO			
Name	Migrant?	Birthplace	Political office(s)
Armstrong, Charles F.	Yes	Statesville, North Carolina	State representative
Blackwell, George W.	Yes	Richmond, Virginia	State representative
Boswell, Paul P.	No	Pittsburgh, Pennsylvania	State representative
Campbell, Kenneth E	No	Kansas City, Kansas	Alderman
Carey, Archibald J., Jr.	No	Chicago, Illinois	Alderman
Carter, James Y.	Yes	Raleigh, North Carolina	State representative
Chew, Charles	Yes	Greenville, Mississippi	Alderman
*Clements, Floy	Yes	Memphis, Tennessee	State representative
Collins, George W.	No	Chicago, Illinois	Alderman
Collins, Otis G.	Yes	Camden, Mississippi	State representative
Conner, Lycurgus J.	No	Chicago, Illinois	State representative
Davis, Corneal A.	Yes	Vicksburg, Mississippi	State representative
Dawson, William L.	Yes	Albany, Georgia	Alderman/congressman
De Priest, Oscar	Yes	Florence, Alabama	Alderman/congressman
Dickerson, Earl B.	Yes	Canton, Mississippi	Alderman
Douglas, Warren B.	No	Fayette, Michigan	State representative
Gaines, Harris B.	Yes	Henderson, Kentucky	State representative
Gardner, J. Horace	No	Cairo, Illinois	State representative
Graham, Elwood	No	Chicago, Illinois	State representative
Grant, Benjamin	No	Chicago, Illinois	Alderman
Greene, Ernest A.	Yes	Rome, Georgia	State representative
Griffin, Charles A.	No	Bellaire, Ohio	State representative
Harewood, Richard A.	No	Barbados, British West Indies	State representative
Harvey, William H.	No	St. Louis, Missouri	Alderman
Holman, Claude W. B.	No	Topeka, Kansas	Alderman
Jackson, Robert R.	No	Malta, Illinois	State representative/ alderman
Jenkins, Charles J.	Yes	Austin, Texas	State representative
Jones, Sidney A.	Yes	Sandersville, Georgia	Alderman
Kersey, George T.	No	Buxton, Canada	State representative
King, William E.	Yes	Oak Ridge, Louisiana	State representative/ state senator
Lewis, Benjamin F.	Yes	Macon, Georgia	Alderman
Lucas, Benjamin H.	No	Brooklyn, Illinois	State representative
Martin, Dudley S.	Yes	Forest Hill, Tennessee	State representative
McLendon, James A.	Yes	Washington, Georgia	State representative
McNairy, Melvin	No	Chicago, Illinois	State representative
Metcalfe, Ralph	Yes	Atlanta, Georgia	Alderman
Miller, Robert H.	Yes	Leesburg, Florida	Alderman
Mitchell, Arthur W.	Yes	Lafayette, Alabama	Congressman

Name	Migrant?	Birthplace	Political office(s)
Partee, Cecil A.	Yes	Blytheville, Arkansas	State representative/ state senator
Roberts, Adelbert H.	No	Vanburen, Michigan	State representative/ state senator
Robinson, William H.	Yes	White Stone, Virginia	State representative
Skyles, Charles M.	Yes	Little Rock, Arkansas	State representative
Smith, Aubrey H.	Yes	Suffok, Virginia	State representative
Smith, Calvin L.	No	Springfield, Ohio	State representative
Smith, Fred J.	Yes	Chattanooga, Tennessee	State representative/ state senator
Torrence, Andrew A.	No	Baltimore, Maryland	State representative
Turner, Sheadrick B.	Yes	West Feliciana, Louisiana	State representative
Wallace, William A.	No	Port DePosite, Maryland	State senator
Warfield, William J.	No	Chicago, Illinois	State representative
Washington, Harold	No	Chicago, Illinois	State representative/ state senator
Welters, Edward A.	Yes	Key West, Florida	State representative
Wilson, Kenneth E.	No	Tacoma, Washington	State representative
Wimbush, Christopher C.	Yes	Atlanta, Georgia	State senator

Source: Compiled by the author.

Note: 53 Black elected officials, 29 migrants.

*Denotes a woman in office.

Notes

Introduction

1. He also taught courses in law as a professor at Shaw University's law school. "A Legal Light" 1904.

2. See *Documenting the American South* 2004.

3. *Grandfather clauses* specified that an individual could vote so long as his grandfather had voted. This requirement put voting out of reach for most Black people, whose grandfathers would not have voted because they were enslaved. Southern Democrats implemented *white primaries*, which refers to their practice of declaring their political party a private organization so that they could exclude Black voters from the most important parts of political participation. Because the Democratic Party was dominant in the South, the person who won the primary election usually went on to win the general election; therefore, the primary election was most important for choosing representatives.

4. This book's analysis ends with the passage of the Voting Rights Act of 1965 as an acknowledgment that Black Americans' interaction with electoral politics changed dramatically after this legislation.

5. Black Americans won election to a wide array of positions between 1915 and 1965. However, I limit my analysis to legislative bodies—boards of aldermen, city councils, state legislatures, and the U.S. House of Representatives—to maintain consistency across the three cities.

Chapter 1

1. "Over the course of their lives, 75 percent of the American population migrate at least once, and many migrate more than once" (Brown 1988: 6).

2. At the national level, Black voters became more consequential because parties and candidates focused on states with large numbers of Electoral College (EC) votes. Migrants frequently went to the largest cities in those states, which had the ability to determine the outcome of the EC vote.

3. Goal alignment could include taking liberal positions on race to demonstrate to white voters that the party was on the same side of an issue as its liberal base.

4. For an excellent overview of Great Migration literature, see Trotter 1991.

5. Maine and Nebraska are exceptions. These states distribute their electors by electoral districts where candidates must win the popular vote to take the districts' EC votes.

6. As Democrats sought to remain competitive, they faced declining shares of the popular vote in presidential elections. Simultaneously, the flood of Black people into the North created an incentive for elites to take liberal positions on race. The recent revisions to the American politics account of this change acknowledge, but do not explore, the connection between the Democratic Party's losses and this mass migration.

7. Although I acknowledge that parties have more considerations than electoral math, the major focus of this book is the impact of a large shift in the population. Therefore, the following analysis focuses on parties' strategic, numerical calculations more than it considers the debates between the party's factions over ideology.

8. Non-immunized citizens are those without political attachments as a result of not having participated in politics in the past.

9. Weiss 1983 makes a similar argument.

10. It is important to keep in mind that Black voters in the South were inactive due to factors that inhibited their participation. They were not inactive in the sense that they could participate but declined to do so.

11. Many European immigrants to America in the post–World War II period entered the system without knowledge of it. For a detailed description of political immunization in immigrant groups, see Andersen 1979.

12. Walton finds that Chicago had high Black representation on the city council, while New York and Detroit were cities with low representation. He finds that that "there are no major differences between the two in regard to improving the social and economic state of blacks within the cities" (1972: 217).

13. Grant 2014.

14. For racial distinctions, the following years distinguish race as Black: 1910, 1920, 1930, and 1970. The years 1940, 1950, and 1960 do not distinguish Black as a separate category. In these instances, it falls under nonwhite: 1940, 1950, and 1960. For 1940 and 1950, the white population is not separated from the total population in the cities.

15. U.S. Census of the Population 1910.

16. Alexander 2008: 51.

17. Du Bois 1920: 757–758.

18. See Nowlin 1931. See also Tatum 1947: 522–533.

19. White 1956: 19.

20. Chuck Stone's and Ronald Walters's theories of Black political participation are helpful frames through which we can interpret the behavior of Black people during this period and others. Later, in the chapters where I describe the political situation in cities, I employ Stone's and Walters's arguments to make sense of the migrants' push for representation in the parties and white politicians' responses to their migration.

21. For a recent study of national politics and the BOP, see Grant, forthcoming.

22. The National Association for the Advancement of Colored People (NAACP) has some estimates for larger cities. However, the source of this information is not specified. Other sources derive the number of Black voters registered in cities or state legislative districts by estimating how many people were registered in predominantly Black precincts.

23. Although the voting age was twenty-one until 1976, I have included all persons ages twenty and older because this is how the Census presents the information for most of the decades under consideration in this book. The Census breaks ages down into five-year increments. I use voting age population as a proxy for the number of Black people with the potential to register and vote because most states did not keep track of race in voter registration data during the period of interest. Because we do not have official voter registration based on race, it is difficult to say with absolute certainty what would have happened with Black voters in an election *before* that election occurred.

24. One of the methodological issues that I mention in this text and grapple with in "Great Migration Politics" (2019) is Moon's inadvertent double counting of Black voters. Using Moon's method, Black voters are the balance of power if there are more of them in the electorate than the margin of victory. However, given that Black people could vote in the North, it is highly likely that Black voters are already among the Democratic and Republican voters in the formula. A better approach would be to separate Black voters out from the total number of voters, determine the margin based on the non-Black vote, and then determine whether Black voters might be able to influence the outcome of the election. It would also be useful to consider the levels at which Black voters may have supported the political parties rather than assume that either party earned 100 percent of the Black vote. As I mention in the earlier part of Chapter 1, it is very difficult to conduct this type of analysis because there is extremely limited information about the race of voters before 1965 and little to no reliable data about who Black voters supported in elections at various levels.

25. The numerical margin is adapted from Moon 1948: 240, app. IV. NUMERICAL MARGIN = (Actual Democratic Vote + Actual Republican Vote)/2 + (1) – Actual number of Republican Votes.

Chapter 2

1. See Johnson and Campbell 1981: 125, 154. See also Gates and Yacavone 2013; Restall 2000.

2. For a comprehensive treatment of the earlier migrations, see Berlin 2010; LaRoche 2014: intro. and chap. 6.

3. Wood 2000: 53–102.

4. See also M. Johnson 1981.

5. Migration to California was a hallmark of the second wave of the migration. Black westward migration did not begin in earnest until internment and did not pick up rapidly until the 1950s.

6. See also White et al. 2005: 215–241. For a detailed consideration of the role of gender in the Great Migration, see Hine 1991.

7. The economic explanation is predominant in the literature. Although understanding what drove Black people to leave the South is important, coming to consensus on the scholarly debate about the factors that drove the Great Migration is outside the scope of this work. Central to my argument is that Black people did decide to leave the South in large numbers and that their decision had a profound impact on the local and national political environments.

8. In the case of California, Black westward migration increased when the U.S. government forced Japanese Americans into internment camps.

9. For an excellent reading about schools in Chicago, see J. Grossman 1989: chap. 9.

10. The Voting Rights Act of 1965 changed the likelihood that Black people could participate in politics regardless of where they lived by creating federal interventions to limit discrimination in political participation on the basis of race throughout the nation.

Chapter 3

1. Detroit Bureau of Governmental Research for the Mayor's Interracial Committee 1926.

2. The city had biennial elections until 1953, when the city charter changed the term to four years.

3. The National Alliance of Postal Employees expanded to include federal employees in 1965 and is now known as the National Alliance of Federal and Postal employees. See https://blackamericaweb.com/2013/08/13/little-known-black-history-fact-national-alliance-of-federal-and-postal-employees/.

4. *Detroit Free Press* 1929.

5. *Detroit Free Press* 1943. See also Martin 1944: 8–10.

6. For another example of strategic voting strategy organized by Black voters in municipal campaigns, see my description of Adam Clayton Powell Jr.'s 1944 election to the city council in New York City.

7. It is important to note that Black people also held other positions in the city and state. I limit my scope to individuals elected to the state legislature and the city council of each city because elected positions vary between cities. Also noteworthy is that some Black elected officials represented jurisdictions right outside the cities under consideration in this work. Because the scope of this book is limited to Detroit, New York, and Chicago, I do not include individuals who held positions in nearby cities in my calculations.

8. See also Warner 1901: 622.

9. *Holland (MI) Evening Sentinel* 1954. See also *Holland (MI) Evening Sentinel* 1961.

10. *Saint Joseph (MI) Herald-Palladium* 1954.

11. *Detroit Free Press* 1959.

12. Cohen 1965.

13. For a thorough description of the interaction of politics and housing activism in Detroit following the Great Migration period, see Shaw 2009.

14. *Lansing (MI) State Journal* 1957.

15. *Detroit Free Press* 1963f.

16. King 1965.

17. *Detroit Free Press* 1962.

18. *Port Huron (MI) Times Herald* 1941.

19. *Lansing (MI) State Journal* 1965b.

20. *Port Huron (MI) Times Herald* 1960.

21. *Lansing (MI) State Journal* 1961.

22. *Holland (MI) Evening Sentinel* 1963.

23. *Lansing (MI) State Journal* 1964.

24. *Holland (MI) Evening Sentinel* 1963.

25. *Lansing (MI) State Journal* 1965a.

26. Toodle 1937: 213–214.

27. Edward Simmons ran in 1943 and finished thirteenth in the field. See Current 1945: 319–321, 332.

28. Hill's campaign manager was Coleman Young, who was a union representative at the time. Young would run unsuccessfully for the city council ten years later. Eventually, he became the first Black mayor of Detroit.

29. Current 1945: 319–321.

30. See Dillard 2007: chap. 4.

31. *Detroit Free Press* 1949.

32. *Detroit Free Press* 1957b.

33. Ibid.

34. *Detroit Free Press* 1957a. Another article reports 142,233 as the vote total: *Detroit Free Press* 1963a.

35. Interestingly, Patrick's father, William T. Patrick Sr., ran for council in 1953 but lost.

36. *Detroit Free Press* 1957c.

37. *Detroit Free Press* 1963a.
38. *Detroit Free Press* 1963b.
39. *Detroit Free Press* 1963e.
40. *Detroit Free Press* 1963f.
41. *Detroit Free Press* 1963c, 1963d.
42. *Detroit Free Press* 1965.

Chapter 4

1. Zora Neale Hurston was born in Notasulga, Alabama, and moved to Florida as a child.

2. Black voters lived in the Eleventh, Thirteenth, Seventeenth, Nineteenth, Twenty-First, and Twenty-Second Assembly Districts.

3. To *crack* a community is to divide the community—in many instances, a like-minded or otherwise similar group of voters—to dilute its voting power. Conversely, *packing* is diluting representation and voting power by cramming groups of voters into a single district rather than distributing them in ways that would maximize their representation.

4. For insightful work on Black ethnics and their political participation, see Greer 2013.

5. *New York Amsterdam News* 1958.

6. The United Colored Democracy (UCD) was an example of Ronald Walters's (1988) dependent-leverage strategy. In this instance, Black New Yorkers were dependent on the Democratic Party for their political access.

7. Black New Yorkers' having the "boldness" to form their own political clubs was characteristic of Walters's (1988: 20) independent-leverage strategy.

8. *New York Age* 1920a.
9. *New York Age* 1917.
10. *New York Amsterdam News* 1925b. See also Grey 1925.
11. *New York Amsterdam News* 1925a.
12. *New York Age* 1925.
13. *New York Amsterdam News* 1933a, 1933b, 1933d.
14. *New York Amsterdam News* 1929a.
15. *New York Amsterdam News* 1933c.
16. *New York Amsterdam News* 1934.
17. Adams 1945.
18. *New York Amsterdam News* 1949.
19. *New York Age* 1945, 1949.
20. *New York Age* 1950b.
21. Booker 1950.
22. *New York Amsterdam News* 1953c.
23. Granger 1953.
24. *New York Amsterdam News* 1953b.
25. Booker 1953.

26. *New York Age* 1959a.

27. The position of municipal judge was of great importance to the Black political class of New York. My discussion of elected officials is limited to individuals who held legislative positions for the sake of parity across the cities under consideration in this book.

28. *New York Legislative Record and Index,* n.d.: 204. See also *Crisis Magazine* 1933: 81.

29. New York State Senate 2014: 4. See also *New York Age* 1919.

30. *New York Amsterdam News* 1929b.

31. *New York Amsterdam News* 1930.

32. *New York Age* 1930.

33. *New York Amsterdam News* 1950.

34. *New York Age* 1955a.

35. *New York Amsterdam News* 1940.

36. *New York Amsterdam Star-News* 1941.

37. The law is named for Irving Ives, a Republican state assemblyman, and Elmer F. Quinn, a Democratic state senator.

38. *Elmira (NY) Star-Gazette* 1945.

39. *New York Age* 1931.

40. *New York Age* 1937.

41. *Binghamton (NY) Press and Sun-Bulletin* 1938.

42. *Rochester (NY) Democrat and Chronicle* 1935.

43. *New York Amsterdam Star-News* 1943.

44. *New York Amsterdam News* 1952.

45. *New York Age* 1935.

46. *New York Age* 1955b.

47. *New York Age*, 1951. See also *New York Age* 1950a.

48. *New York Amsterdam News* 1959.

49. *New York Age* 1958.

50. *New York Age* 1959b.

51. *New York Amsterdam News* 1964.

52. Although not a migrant, Adam Clayton Powell is very important to Black politics in New York City. For a thorough reading about his life, see Hamilton 1992.

53. John M. Royall had a noteworthy campaign for a seat on the board of aldermen in 1913.

54. *New York Age* 1920c, 1921.

55. *New York Age* 1920b.

56. *New York Age* 1924a.

57. *New York Amsterdam News* 1951.

58. The other councilmen were Jack Sharkey and Stanley Isaacs.

59. *New-York Tribune* 1921.

60. *New York Age* 1929.

61. *New York Amsterdam News* 1953a.

62. *New York Daily News* 1959.

63. *New York Age* 1924b.

64. *New York Amsterdam News* 1928.

Chapter 5

1. Lines were redrawn in 1931. Black people were limited to the Second and Third Wards because Louis B. Anderson and Robert Jackson worked to preserve their seats and packed Black voters into two wards instead of distributing them in a way that might have contributed to the election of a third Black alderman (Wilson 1960: 77).

2. *Chicago Tribune* 1924.

3. *Chicago Defender* 1931.

4. Doherty 1952.

5. Fields 1933.

6. *Chicago Defender* 1943.

7. *Chicago Tribune* 1947.

8. Hirsch 1995, citing the *Chicago Defender*, March 22 and 29, 1947.

9. Coleman 1963.

10. *Chicago Defender* 1955.

11. These data begin at 1919 because I am unable to attain the voting returns for the 1915 mayoral elections.

12. *Chicago Defender* 1958.

13. Marilou Hedlund, a white Chicagoan, was also elected to the city council in the 1971 election.

14. *Chicago Defender* 1956.

15. *Norfolk (VA) New Journal and Guide* 1924.

16. *Chicago Tribune* 1941.

17. *Chicago Defender* 1939.

18. *Chicago Defender* 1941b.

19. *Chicago Tribune* 1963b. See also *Chicago Tribune* 1965.

20. *Chicago Defender* 1941a.

21. *Chicago Tribune* 1961b. For a detailed description of Fair Employment Practices Committee (FEPC) laws in Illinois, see Chen 2009.

22. Osby 1963.

23. *New York Amsterdam News* 1927.

24. *Chicago Defender* 1927.

25. *Chicago Tribune* 1959.

26. *Chicago Tribune* 1963d.

27. *Chicago Tribune* 1963c.

28. One year earlier, Jackson—a Black alderman elected from the Second District—had been successful in convincing the city council to pass legislation that would prevent individuals in parades from wearing masks. On the effort in the state legislature, see *Chicago Defender* 1923.

29. *Chicago Defender* 1935.

30. *Decatur (IL) Daily Review* 1946.

31. *Chicago Defender* 1959. The Sixth Ward changed, changing the face of its representative. The number of white voters in the ward had decreased to about 10 percent by 1959. In 1948, the ward was only half Black. The ward was 40 percent white when Robert Miller won election in 1959, following Sidney Jones, who had held the position since 1955.

32. *Chicago Defender* 1961.

33. *Chicago Tribune* 1964.

34. *Chicago Defender* 1948.

35. *Chicago Defender* 1960.

36. *Chicago Tribune* 1961a.

37. *Chicago Defender* 1963.

38. *Chicago Tribune* 1963a.

39. *Chicago Defender* 1945.

40. *Chicago Defender* 1940a.

41. *Chicago Defender* 1940b. See also J. Johnson 1942: 8; *DeKalb (IL) Daily Chronicle* 1965.

42. *Chicago Defender* 1965a.

43. *Chicago Defender* 1965b.

44. Slaughter 1962. See also *Chicago Tribune* 1962.

45. *Decatur (IL) Daily Review* 1962.

46. During Reconstruction, a number of Black people served in the U.S. Congress, representing districts in the South where they had large numbers and where the bulk of the Black population lived.

47. Field 1962.

Conclusion

1. Two other mayors outside the South—Melvin W. Carter III, of St. Paul, Minnesota, and Wilmot Collins, of Helena, Montana—became the first Black mayors in their cities during this election.

2. Charles 2018.

References

Adams, J. J. 1945. "O'Dwyer Has Victory in Landslide." *New York Amsterdam News*, November 10.

Alexander, Shawn Leigh. 2008. *T. Thomas Fortune, the Afro-American Agitator: A Collection of Writings, 1880–1928*. Gainesville: University Press of Florida.

Ali, Omar H. 2008. *In the Balance of Power: Independent Black Politics and Third-Party Movements in the United States*. Athens: Ohio University Press.

Allswang, John M. 1977. *Bosses, Machines, and Urban Voters: An American Symbiosis*. Port Washington, NY: Kennikat Press.

Andersen, Kristi. 1979. *The Creation of a Democratic Majority, 1928–1936*. Chicago: University of Chicago Press.

Barnard, Harry. 2002. *Independent Man: The Life of Senator James Couzens*. Detroit: Wayne State University Press.

Bates, Beth Tompkins. 2012. *The Making of Black Detroit in the Age of Henry Ford*. Chapel Hill: University of North Carolina Press.

Bawn, Kathleen, Martin Cohen, David Karol, Seth Masket, Hans Noel, and John Zaller. 2012. "A Theory of Political Parties: Groups, Policy Demands and Nominations in American Politics." *Perspectives on Politics* 10 (3): 571–597.

Berlin, Ira. 2010. *The Making of African America: The Four Great Migrations*. New York: Penguin.

Biles, Roger. 1984. *Big City Boss in Depression and War: Mayor Edward J. Kelly of Chicago*. DeKalb: Northern Illinois University Press.

———. 1995. "Edward J. Kelly: New Deal Machine Builder." In *The Mayors: The Chicago Political Tradition*, ed. Paul M. Green and Melvin Holli, 111–125. Carbondale: Southern Illinois University Press.

Binghamton (NY) Press and Sun-Bulletin. 1938. "Police Protest Bill on Arrest." *Binghamton (NY) Press and Sun-Bulletin*, February 23.

Biondi, Martha. 2003. *To Stand and Fight: The Struggle for Civil Rights in Postwar New York*. Cambridge, MA: Harvard University Press.

Black, Earl, and Merle Black. 2002. *The Rise of Southern Republicans*. Cambridge, MA: Harvard University Press.

Blackett, Richard J. M. 2013. *Making Freedom: The Underground Railroad and the Politics of Slavery*. Chapel Hill: University of North Carolina Press.

Blakely, Robert J., and Marcus Shepard. 2006. *Earl B. Dickerson: A Voice for Freedom and Equality*. Evanston, IL: Northwestern University Press.

Bontemps, Arna W., and Jack Contemps. 1966. *Anyplace but Here*. New York: Hill and Wang.

Booker, J. 1950. "Acting Mayor Vincent Impellitteri in Midst of 'Poor Man's Campaign.'" *New York Amsterdam News*, October 21.

———. 1953. "Wagner, Jack Combo Pledges 'New Deal.'" *New York Amsterdam News*, November 7.

Brooks, Thomas R. 1974. *Walls Come Tumbling Down: A History of the Civil Rights Movement, 1940–1970*. Englewood Cliffs, NJ: Prentice-Hall.

Brown, Thad A. 1988. *Migration and Politics: The Impact of Population Mobility on American Voting Behavior*. Chapel Hill: University of North Carolina Press.

Bunche, Ralph. 1929. "The Thompson-Negro Alliance." *Opportunity* 7 (March): 78. Cahill, Barry. 1999. "The Black Loyalist Myth in Atlantic Canada." *Acadiensis* 29 (1): 76–87.

Campbell, Angus, Philip Converse, Warren Miller, and Donald Stokes. 1960. *The American Voter*. Chicago: University of Chicago Press.

Capeci, Dominic J. 1977. *The Harlem Riot of 1943*. Philadelphia: Temple University Press.

Carmines, Edward G., and James A. Stimson. 1989. *Issue Evolution: Race and the Transformation of American Politics*. Princeton, NJ: Princeton University Press.

Charles, J. Brian. 2018. "For New Generation of Black Mayors, Focus Is on Balance." Governing the States and Localities. June 14. www.governing.com/topics/politics/gov-black-mayors-lc.html.

Chavis, J. M. T. 1970. "James Couzens: Mayor of Detroit, 1919–1922." Ph.D. diss., Michigan State University.

Chen, Anthony S. 2009. *The Fifth Freedom: Jobs, Politics, and Civil Rights in the United States, 1941–1972*. Princeton, NJ: Princeton University Press.

Chicago Defender. 1923. "Roberts' Klan Bill Passes in Illinois House: Chicago Man's Measure Carries 107–3." *Chicago Defender*, April 28.

———. 1927. "Illinois Legislature Hits Color Issue: Small Signs Two Jim Crow House Bills Hospitals and Schools under Ban." *Chicago Defender*, July 16.

———. 1931. "Democratic Landslide Beats Thompson." *Chicago Defender*, April 11.

———. 1935. "State Urges Anti-lynching Legislation." *Chicago Defender*, February 16.

———. 1939. "Citizens Laud Achievements of Law Makers: 61st General Assembly of Illinois Makes New History." *Chicago Defender*, July 15.

———. 1940a. "Demand Race Be Given 'L' Bus, Street Car Jobs: New Job Drive Council Committee Hears Demand for Race Jobs." *Chicago Defender*, July 6.

———. 1940b. "The Unified Traction Ordinance." *Chicago Defender*, August 24.

———. 1941a. "Assembly Ends Heated Session; Bills Aid Race." *Chicago Defender*, July 12.

———. 1941b. "Wallace's Senate Record Shows He 'Keeps Faith.'" *Chicago Defender*, July 19.

———. 1943. "De Priest Back as Alderman—Harvey Wins: Kelly Carries South Side after McKibbin's Stand on Covenants Is Bared." *Chicago Defender*, April 17.

———. 1945. "Chicago City Council Outlaws Job Prejudice." *Chicago Defender*, September 1.

———. 1948. "Carey Sponsors Law against Biased Housing: 12 Other Aldermen Lend Support to Proposed Ordinance." *Chicago Defender*, September 25.

———. 1955. "Chicago Gets Fifth Alderman, Aids Daley." *Chicago Defender*, April 16.

———. 1956. "Chicago Sends Largest Delegation to Capital: 10 Now in Ill. State Assembly." *Chicago Defender*, November 17.

———. 1958. "Civil Rights, Aim of Woman Solon." *Chicago Defender*, November 22.

———. 1959. "Kenneth Campbell Makes History in City Council." *Chicago Defender*, May 11.

———. 1960. "City Council Approves Study of Housing Bias." *Chicago Defender*, November 28.

———. 1961. "Aldermen Split over Cop Bill." *Chicago Defender*, March 2.

———. 1963. "City Council Passes Housing Bill, 30–16." *Chicago Defender*, September 12.

———. 1965a. "Alderman Views Controversy—Chicago Style." *Chicago Defender*, February 6.

———. 1965b. "Sen. Fred Smith Hits GOP Illiterate Voters' Bill." *Chicago Defender*, May 3.

Chicago Tribune. 1924. "Dever Welcomes Colored Convention Delegate." *Chicago Tribune*, February 13.

———. 1941. "Slum Clearing Bill Changes in Legislature." *Chicago Tribune*, April 16.

———. 1947. "GOP Confident of Big Gains in Council Today." *Chicago Tribune*, February 25.

———. 1959. "Bill to Curb Segregation Here Passed." *Chicago Tribune*, April 16.

———. 1961a. "Fair Housing Stirs Debate by Aldermen." *Chicago Tribune*, March 28.

———. 1961b. "House Sends FEPC Bill to Gov. Kerner." *Chicago Tribune*, June 30.

———. 1962. "Bar 25 Medics from Caring for Reliefers." *Chicago Tribune*, June 30.

———. 1963a. "Councilmen Vote 30–16 in Hot Session." *Chicago Tribune*, September 12.

———. 1963b. "Open Housing Bill Killed in Illinois House." *Chicago Tribune*, June 21.

———. 1963c. "Police Arrest Five in School Disorder." *Chicago Tribune*, September 6.

———. 1963d. "Wakegan School Board Names Racial Study Unit." *Chicago Tribune*, July 18.

———. 1964. "Aldermen Praise Neighborhood Groups." *Chicago Tribune*, March 12.

———. 1965. "Senate Group to Vote Tuesday on 4 Bills." *Chicago Tribune*, June 6.

Ciment, James. 2007. *Atlas of African-American History*. New York: Infobase Publishing.

Cohen, Hal. 1965. "Revolt Wins Shift in Slum Clearing." *Detroit Free Press*, April 6.

Coleman, T. 1963. "Negro Vote Credited for Daley Victory." *Chicago Defender*, April 4.

Converse, Philip E. 1966. "The Concept of the Normal Vote." In *Elections and the Public Order*, ed. Angus Campbell, 9–39. New York: Wiley.

Countryman, Matthew J. 2007. *Up South: Civil Rights and Black Power in Philadelphia*. Philadelphia: University of Pennsylvania Press.

Crisis Magazine. 1933. "The Life Work of Edward A. Johnson." *Crisis Magazine*, April, 81.

Current, G. "The Detroit Election: Problem in Reconversion." *Crisis Magazine*, November 1945, 319–332.

Decatur (IL) Daily Review. 1946. "Charges Klan Active Here." *Decatur (IL) Daily Review*, August 1.

———. 1962. "Kerner, Legislature Take Negative Approach to Welfare, Ex-IPAC Chief Martin Contends." *Decatur (IL) Daily Review*, August 26.

DeKalb (IL) Daily Chronicle. 1965. "Legislation Stirs Clash." *DeKalb (IL) Daily Chronicle*, June 11.

Detroit Bureau of Governmental Research for the Mayor's Interracial Committee. 1926. *The Negro in Detroit*.

Detroit Free Press. 1929. "Race Question Is Brought Up: Bowles Men Circulate Copies of Negro Paper; Smith Aide Deplores Issue." *Detroit Free Press*, November 4.

———. 1943. "Housing Body Bars Bi-Racial Occupancy." *Detroit Free Press*, April 30.

———. 1949. "Election Results." *Detroit Free Press*, November 9.

———. 1957a. "City Ballot." *Detroit Free Press*, November 6.

———. 1957b. "Final Election Returns." *Detroit Free Press*, September 12.

———. 1957c. "Patrick Won't Be Negro Watchdog." *Detroit Free Press*, November 7.

———. 1959. "Urge Teeth in Rights Law." *Detroit Free Press*, March 11.

———. 1962. "Measure Passed by 81–6 Vote: Woman Legislator Says It Won't Help." *Detroit Free Press*, March 3.

———. 1963a. "Bill Patrick: He Labors to Help Negroes Progress." *Detroit Free Press*, July 29.

———. 1963b. "Colleagues Praise Patrick's Work." *Detroit Free Press*, December 6.

———. 1963c. "Councilmen Name Patrick for Top Supervisor Job." *Detroit Free Press*, April 3.

———. 1963d. "Council Stunned: Why Patrick Quit. He Wants to Return to Law. Will Join Staff of Michigan Bell." *Detroit Free Press*, December 6.

———. 1963e. "1963—The Year of Historic Moments." *Detroit Free Press*, December 29.

———. 1963f. "Olsen Denies Plea for New Probe in Scott Shooting." *Detroit Free Press*, July 16.

———. 1965. "Poindexter: The Last Hurrah. Hood: The First Hurrah." *Detroit Free Press*, November 4.

Dillard, Angela D. 2007. *Faith in the City: Preaching Radical Social Change in Detroit*. Ann Arbor: University of Michigan Press.

Documenting the American South. 2004. University Library, University of North Carolina at Chapel Hill. http://docSouth.unc.edu/church/johnson/bio.html#titles_by_author. Accessed December 13, 2016.

Doherty, J. 1952. "John Stege, Fighting Cop." *Chicago Tribune*, May 25.

Downs, Anthony. 1957. *An Economic Theory of Democracy*. New York: Harper.

Drake, Saint C., and Horace R. Cayton. 1962. *Black Metropolis: A Study of Negro Life in a Northern City*. New York: Harper and Row.

Du Bois, W. E. B. 1920. "The Republicans and the Black Voter." *Nation Magazine* 110, no. 2866 (June 5): 757–758.

Elmira (NY) Star-Gazette. 1945. "Assembly Passes Ives Quinn Bill, 109–32." *Elmira (NY) Star-Gazette*, March 1.

Erie, Steven P. 1990. *Rainbow's End: Irish-Americans and the Dilemmas of Urban Machine Politics, 1840–1985*. Vol. 15. Berkeley: University of California Press.

Feinstein, Brian D., and Eric Schickler. 2008. "Platforms and Partners: The Civil Rights Realignment Reconsidered." *Studies in American Political Development* 22 (1): 1–31.

Field, K. C. 1962. "Bill Dawson: 'The Quiet Man.'" *Chicago Defender*, September 22.

Fields, A. N. 1933. "City Mourns at Bier of Mayor Anton Cermak." *Chicago Defender*, March 11.

Fine, Sidney. 1973. *Frank Murphy: The Detroit Years*. Ann Arbor: University of Michigan Press.

Flamming, Douglas. 2005. *Bound for Freedom: Black Los Angeles in Jim Crow America.* Berkeley: University of California Press.

Fox, Craig. 2011. *Everyday Klansfolk: White Protestant Life and the KKK in 1920s Michigan.* East Lansing: Michigan State University Press.

Fragnoli, Raymond R. 1982. *The Transformation of Reform: Progressivism in Detroit—and After, 1912–1933.* New York: Garland Publishing.

Frendreis, John P. 1989. "Migration as a Source of Changing Party Strength." *Social Science Quarterly* 70 (1): 211–220.

Furniss, George Martin. 1969. "The Political Assimilation of Negroes in New York City." Ph.D. diss., Columbia University.

Garrett, Charles. 1961. *The La Guardia Years: Machine and Reform Politics in New York City.* New Brunswick: Rutgers University Press.

Gates, Henry Louis, Jr., and Donald Yacovone. 2013. *The African Americans: Many Rivers to Cross.* Carlsbad, CA: Smiley Books.

Goodwin, E. Marvin. 1990. *Black Migration in America from 1915 to 1960: An Uneasy Exodus.* Vol. 3. Lewiston, NY: Edwin Mellen Press.

Gordon, Rita Werner. 1969. "The Change in the Political Alignment of Chicago's Negroes during the New Deal." *Journal of American History* 56 (3): 584–603.

Gosnell, Harold Foote. 1967. *Negro Politicians: The Rise of Negro Politicians in Chicago.* Chicago: University of Chicago Press.

Gottlieb, Peter. 1996. *Making Their Own Way: Southern Blacks' Migration to Pittsburgh, 1916–30.* Vol. 82. Urbana: University of Illinois Press.

Granger, B. 1953. "Hulan Jack Helps Wagner Win City." *New York Amsterdam News*, September 19.

Grant, Keneshia. 2014. "Relocation and Realignment: How the Great Migration Changed the Face of the Democratic Party." Ph.D. diss., Syracuse University.

———. Forthcoming. "Great Migration Politics: The Impact of the Great Migration on Democratic Presidential Election Campaigns from 1948–1960." *Du Bois Review* 16 (1).

Greenberg, Cheryl. 1997. *"Or Does It Explode?": Black Harlem in the Great Depression.* New York: Oxford University Press.

Greer, Christina M. 2013. *Black Ethnics: Race, Immigration, and the Pursuit of the American Dream.* New York: Oxford University Press.

Gregory, James N. 2006. *The Southern Diaspora: How the Great Migrations of Black and White Southerners Transformed America.* Chapel Hill: University of North Carolina Press.

Grey, E. M. 1925. "The Political Situation Tense." *New York Amsterdam News*, September 2.

Grimshaw, William J. 1992. *Bitter Fruit: Black Politics and the Chicago Machine, 1931–1991.* Chicago: University of Chicago Press.

Grossman, James R. 1989. *Land of Hope: Chicago, Black Southerners, and the Great Migration.* Chicago: University of Chicago Press.

Hamilton, Charles V. 1992. *The Political Biography of an American Dilemma.* New York: Atheneum.

Harris, Fredrick. 2012. *The Price of the Ticket: Barack Obama and the Rise and Decline of Black Politics.* Oxford, UK: Oxford University Press.

Hellwig, David J. 1981. "Black Leaders and United States Immigration Policy, 1917–1929." *Journal of Negro History* 66 (2): 110–127.

Hine, Darlene C. 1991. "Black Migration to the Urban Midwest: The Gender Dimension, 1915–1945." In *The Great Migration in Historical Perspectives: New Dimensions of Race, Class, and Gender*, ed. William Trotter Jr., 127–146. Bloomington: Indiana University Press.

Hirsch, Arnold R. 1995. "Martin H. Kennelly: The Mugwump and the Machine." In *The Mayors: The Chicago Political Tradition*, ed. Paul M. Green and Melvin G. Hilli, 126–143. Carbondale: Southern Illinois University Press.

———. 2009. *Making the Second Ghetto: Race and Housing in Chicago 1940–1960.* Chicago: University of Chicago Press.

Holland (MI) Evening Sentinel. 1954. "Power to Subpoena Persons, Records Erased from Bill: Group Will Not Have Enforcement Power, but Can Hear Evidence." *Holland (MI) Evening Sentinel*, March 5.

———. 1961. "Bill Would Provide Cash for Buildings." *Holland (MI) Evening Sentinel*, January 13.

———. 1963. "Legislator Hopes to Aid Migrant Group." *Holland (MI) Evening Sentinel*, March 7.

Holley, Donald. 2000. *Black Migration, and How They Shaped the Modern South.* Fayetteville: University of Arkansas Press.

James, Scott C. 2006. *Presidents, Parties, and the State: A Party System Perspective on Democratic Regulatory Choice, 1884–1936.* New York: Cambridge University Press.

Johnson, Daniel Milo, and Rex R. Campbell. 1981. *Black Migration in America: A Social Demographic History.* Durham, NC: Duke University Press.

Johnson, Edward A. 1942. "A Student at Atlanta University." *Phylon (1940–1956)* 3 (2): 135–148. doi:10.2307/271521.

Johnson, Michael P. 1981. "Runaway Slaves and the Slave Communities in South Carolina, 1799 to 1830." *William and Mary Quarterly: A Magazine of Early American History* 38 (3): 418–441.

Karol, Davis. 2009. *Party Position Change in American Politics: Coalition Management.* New York: Cambridge University Press.

Katzman, David M. 1973. *Before the Ghetto: Black Detroit in the Nineteenth Century.* Urbana: University of Illinois Press.

Katznelson, Ira. 1973. *Black Men, White Cities: Race, Politics, and Migration in the United States, 1900–30 and Britain, 1948–68.* New York: Oxford University Press.

Keiser, Richard A. 1997. *Subordination or Empowerment? African-American Leadership and the Struggle for Urban Political Power.* New York: Oxford University Press.

Kersten, Andrew Edmund. 1998. "Fighting for Fair Employment: The FEPC in the Midwest, 1941–1946." Ph.D. diss., University of Cincinnati.

Key, Vladimer O., Jr. 1955. "A Theory of Critical Elections." *Journal of Politics* 17 (1): 3–18.

———. 1959. "Secular Realignment and the Party System." *Journal of Politics* 21 (2): 198–210.

King, Bill. 1965. "Senator Basil Brown Sponsors 75 before Filing Deadline." *Lansing (MI) State Journal*, April 18.

Lansing (MI) State Journal. 1957. "Ask Probe of Prison: Inhuman Practices Are Alleged at Detroit Institution." *Lansing (MI) State Journal*, May 10.

———. 1961. "Migrant Farm Worker Is Legislative Issue." *Lansing (MI) State Journal*, April 19.

———. 1964. "Migration Labor Problem Largely Ignored in the State." *Lansing (MI) State Journal*, September 29.

———. 1965a. "Farm Labor Probed by Governor." *Lansing (MI) State Journal*, February 24.

———. 1965b. "House Moves to Erase Driver License Photos, Then Reneges." *Lansing (MI) State Journal*, May 19.

LaRoche, Cheryl Janifer. 2014. *Free Black Communities and the Underground Railroad: The Geography of Resistance*. Urbana: University of Illinois Press.

Lemann, Nicholas. 1992. *The Promised Land: The Great Black Migration and How it Changed America*. New York: Vintage.

Levine, David A. 1976. *Internal Combustion: The Races in Detroit, 1915–1926*. Westport, CT: Greenwood Press.

Lewinson, Edwin R. 1974. *Black Politics in New York City*. New York: Twayne Publishers.

Marks, Carole. 1989. *Farewell—We're Good and Gone: The Great Black Migration*. Bloomington: Indiana University Press.

Martin, Louis E. 1944. "Detroit—Still Dynamite." *Crisis Magazine* 51 (1): 8–10.

McNickle, Chris. 1993. *To Be Mayor of New York: Ethnic Politics in the City*. New York: Columbia University Press.

McPhee, William N., and Jack Ferguson. 1962. *Public Opinion and Congressional Elections*. New York: Free Press of Glencoe.

Meier, August, and Elliott M. Rudwick. 1979. *Black Detroit and the Rise of the UAW*. Ann Arbor: University of Michigan Press.

Moon, Henry Lee. 1948. *Balance of Power: The Negro Vote*. Garden City, NY: Double Day.

New York Age. 1917. "What Fusion Has Done." *New York Age*, October 25.

———. 1919. "News of Greater New York." *New York Age*, January 11.

———. 1920a. "Bath House Hearing Friday at City Hall." *New York Age*, July 17.

———. 1920b. "Charles Roberts Bath House Legislation." *New York Age*, July 17.

———. 1920c. "Roberts Advocates for a Public Bath House in Harlem." *New York Age*, May 22.

———. 1921. "Harlem Bath House Plans Submitted to Ald. Roberts." *New York Age*, August 20.

———. 1924a. "Alderman John W. Smith Wins Relief for a Tenant by Board of Health Action." *New York Age*, June 28.

———. 1924b. "Republicans Designate Negro as Candidate for Nomination to Congress from New York." *New York Age*, August 16.

———. 1925. "Republican Candidates Knifed by Voters in 'Hill' Districts." *New York Age*, November 21.

———. 1929. "North Harlem to Have New Medical Center Soon through the Efforts of Dr. Wynne, Mayor Walker, Ald. Moore." *New York Age*, October 26.

———. 1930. "Digest of Record of Legislative Bills Affecting Harlem Community in the Past 12 Years." *New York Age*, May 10.

———. 1931. "Brooklyn Meeting Protests the Failure of Stephen's Bill." *New York Age*, May 23.

———. 1935. "Governor Curbs School Jim Crow: Signs Bill to Prevent Discrimination in Public Schools." *New York Age*, May 11.

———. 1937. "Players to Be Exempt from Arrest." *New York Age*, February 20.

———. 1945. "The Mayoralty Election." *New York Age*, November 17.

———. 1949. "Why We Are for Re-Election of Mayor O'Dwyer." *New York Age*, October 15.

———. 1950a. "Assemblyman Thomas Dickens Commended in Representation of the Eleventh District." *New York Age*, March 11.

———. 1950b. "Impy Slams Bias, Vows Fair Shuffle." *New York Age*, November 4.

———. 1951. "Assemblyman in Action." *New York Age*, March 10.

———. 1955a. "The New York State Committee on Discrimination in Housing." *New York Age*, October 15.

———. 1955b. Zaretski and Buchanan Bills Hit Surety Bans." *New York Age*, January 22.

———. 1958. "Migrant Workers to Be Protected." *New York Age*, July 12.

———. 1959a. "Harlem Hospital Opening." *New York Age*, August 1.

———. 1959b. "Watson, Dickens, Back Bills Helping Migrants." *New York Age*, March 7.

New York Amsterdam News. 1925a. "Five Great Issues in This Campaign." *New York Amsterdam News*, November 4.

———. 1925b. "New York Mayoralty Election." *New York Amsterdam News*, May 27.

———. 1927. "Ill. Bill Penalizing Jim Crow Schools: South African Leader in London." *New York Amsterdam News*, July 27.

———. 1928. "A Negro for Congress." *New York Amsterdam News*, March 21.

———. 1929a. "Election Day." *New York Amsterdam News*, October 30.

———. 1929b. "Harlem's Assemblymen-Elect." *New York Amsterdam News*, December 25.

———. 1930. "Tenant Stay Bill Passes Assembly." *New York Amsterdam News*, March 12.

———. 1933a. "De Priest Will Aid La Guardia Monday." *New York Amsterdam News*, October 25.

———. 1933b. "La Guardia Friend of Negro, De Priest Says." *New York Amsterdam News*, November 1.
———. 1933c. "La Guardia Takes Harlem." *New York Amsterdam News*, November 8.
———. 1933d. "Political Pie." *New York Amsterdam News*, October 18.
———. 1934. "Thank You, Mr. Mayor." *New York Amsterdam News*, September 29.
———. 1940. "Andrews Introduces Bills to Curb Bias." *New York Amsterdam News*, January 13.
———. 1949. "Harlem May Decide City Election." *New York Amsterdam News*, November 5.
———. 1950. "Pinckney Polls Voters' Wants." *New York Amsterdam News*, December 16.
———. 1951. "Earl Brown Hits Housing Dilemma." *New York Amsterdam News*, May 19.
———. 1952. "Archibald's Senate Fight Causes Split in Tammany." *New York Amsterdam News*, July 12.
———. 1953a. "Brown Bill to Probe Police Passes Council." *New York Amsterdam News*, May 16.
———. 1953b. "Wagner Pledges to Work with Leaders." *New York Amsterdam News*, October 31.
———. 1953c. "Wagner Vows End to Bias in Housing." *New York Amsterdam News*, August 29.
———. 1958. "Dickens Opens Drive in Assembly Race." *New York Amsterdam News*, July 5.
———. 1959. "Migrant Labor Bill before Legislature." *New York Amsterdam News*, January 17.
———. 1964. "Ask Migrant Camps Be Shut Down." *New York Amsterdam News*, August 29.
New York Amsterdam Star-News. 1941. "Harlem Assemblymen Spur Movement to Air Racial Discrimination in State." *New York Amsterdam Star-News*, March 1.
———. 1943. "Andrews Demands Harlem Senate District: Explains Vote Against Bill." *New York Amsterdam Star-News*, March 27.
New York Daily News. 1959. "Mayor Rallies Youth Offices to Curb Crime." *New York Daily News*, September 1.
New York Legislative Record and Index. n.d. Albany, NY: Legislative Index.
New York State Senate. 2014. "A Look at the History of the Legislators of Color: 1917–2014." New York State Black, Puerto Rican, Hispanic, and Asian Legislative Caucus, 4. https://www.nysenate.gov/newsroom/articles/1917-2014-look-history-legislators-color.
New-York Tribune. 1921. "Graft and Misrule Charged against Harlem Hospital." *New-York Tribune*, February 28.
Nordin, Dennis Sven, 1997. *The New Deal's Black Congressman: A Life of Arthur Wergs Mitchell*. Columbia: University of Missouri Press.
Norfolk (VA) New Journal and Guide. 1924. "Race Man Wins in Election

to Ill. State Senate." *Norfolk (VA) New Journal and Guide*, November 1.

Nowlin, William Felbert. 1931. *The Negro in American National Politics.* Boston: Stratford.

Orr, Marion Everett. 1993. "Black Political Incorporation—Phase Two: The Cases of Baltimore and Detroit." Ph.D. diss., University of Maryland, College Park.

Osby, S. B. 1963. "Sen. Smith Pushes Bill Banning State Job Bias." *Chicago Defender*, February 2.

Osofsky, Gilbert, 1971. *Harlem: The Making of a Ghetto: Negro New York, 1890–1930.* New York: Harper and Row.

Painter, Nell, 1977. *Exodusters: Black Migration to Kansas after Reconstruction.* New York: Knopf.

———. 1991. "Foreword." In *The Great Migration in Historical Perspective: New Dimensions of Race, Class, and Gender*, ed. Joe William Trotter Jr., viii–x. Bloomington: Indiana University Press.

Petrocik, John R., 1981. *Party Coalitions: Realignment and the Decline of the New Deal Party System.* Chicago: University of Chicago Press.

Port Huron (MI) Times Herald. 1941. "Urges Lobbyists to Be Restricted to Prevent Bribery." *Port Huron (MI) Times Herald*, March 21.

———. 1960. "Migratory Labor Study Asked." *Port Huron (MI) Times Herald*, February 5.

Powell, William S., ed. 1980. *Dictionary of North Carolina Biography.* Chapel Hill: University of North Carolina Press.

Rakove, Milton L. 1976. *Don't Make No Waves . . . Don't Back No Losers: An Insiders' Analysis of the Daley Machine.* Bloomington: Indiana University Press.

Restall, Matthew. 2000. "Black Conquistadors: Armed Africans in Early Spanish America." *The Americas* 57 (2): 171–205.

Rich, Wilbur C. 1989. *Coleman Young and Detroit Politics: From Social Activist to Power Broker.* Detroit: Wayne State University Press.

Rochester (NY) Democrat and Chronicle. 1935. "Test Vote Hits Redistrict Bill in Assembly." *Rochester (NY) Democrat and Chronicle*, March 22.

Rogers, Reuel R. 2006. *Afro-Caribbean Immigrants and the Politics of Incorporation: Ethnicity, Exception, or Exit.* Cambridge, UK: Cambridge University Press.

Saint Joseph (MI) Herald-Palladium. 1954. "Dems Pass Senate FEPC Bill: Democrats Claim Heart of Measure Cut Out; Goes to House for Vote." *Saint Joseph (MI) Herald-Palladium*, March 5.

Schattschneider, Elmer. 1942. *Party Government: American Government in Action.* New York: Farrar and Rinehart.

Scheiner, Seth M. 1965. *Negro Mecca: A History of the Negro in New York City, 1865–1920.* New York: New York University Press.

Schickler, Eric. 2016. *Racial Realignment: The Transformation of American Liberalism, 1932–1965.* Princeton, NJ: Princeton University Press.

Schmidt, John R. 1989. *The Mayor Who Cleaned Up Chicago: A Political Biography of William E. Dever.* DeKalb: Northern Illinois University Press.

Scott, Emmett Jay. 1920. *Negro Migration during the War.* New York: Oxford University Press.

Shaw, Todd C. 2009. *Now Is the Time! Detroit Black Politics and Grassroots Activism.* Durham, NC: Duke University Press.

Sides, Josh. 2004. *L.A. City Limits: African American Los Angeles from the Great Depression to the Present.* Berkeley: University of California Press.

Slaughter, A. J. 1962. "Leaders in Uproar over Welfare Cuts." *Chicago Defender*, July 2.

Smith, Carl O., and Stephen B. Sarasohn. 1946. "Recent Mayoralty Elections: Hate Propaganda in Detroit." *Public Opinion Quarterly* 10 (1): 24–52.

Spear, Allan H. 1967. *Black Chicago: The Making of a Negro Ghetto, 1890–1920.* Chicago: University of Chicago Press.

Stone, Chuck. 1970. *Black Political Power in America.* New York: Dell Publishing.

Stovall, A. J. 1983. "Before Coleman Young: The Growth of the Detroit Black Elected Officialdom." Ph.D. diss., Union Graduate School, Cincinnati.

Sugrue, Thomas J. 1995. "Crabgrass-Roots Politics: Race, Rights, and the Reaction against Liberalism in the Urban North, 1940–1964." *Journal of American History* 82 (2): 551–578.

———. 2008. *Sweet Land of Liberty: The Forgotten Struggle for Civil Rights in the North.* New York: Random House.

———. 2014. *The Origins of the Urban Crisis: Race and Inequality in Postwar Detroit.* Princeton, NJ: Princeton University Press.

Tatum, E. L. 1947. "The Changed Political Thought of the Negro." *Journal of Negro Education* 16, no. 4 (Autumn): 522–533.

Thomas, Richard W. 1992. *Life for Us Is What We Make It: Building Black Community in Detroit, 1915—1945.* Bloomington: Indiana University Press.

Thompson, Heather Ann. 2001. *Whose Detroit? Politics, Labor, and Race in a Modern American City.* Ithaca, NY: Cornell University Press.

Toodle, A. C. 1937. "The Negro in Michigan Politics." *Crisis Magazine*, July, 213-214.

Travis, Dempsey. 1987. *An Autobiography of Black Politics.* Chicago: Urban Research Press.

Trotter, Joe W., ed. 1991. *The Great Migration in Historical Perspective: New Dimensions of Race, Class, and Gender.* Bloomington: Indiana University Press.

Turrini, Joseph, 1999. "Phooie on Louie: African American Detroit and the Election of Jerry Cavanagh." *Michigan History Magazine* (November/December): 11–17.

U.S. Census Bureau. 1910. "State of Birth of the Native Population: 1910." Chapter 6 of *Detailed Characteristics of the Population*. https://www.census.gov/library/publications/1913/dec/vol-1-population.html.

———. 1940. *Detailed Characteristics of the Population*. https://www.census.gov/library/publications/1943/dec/population-vol-2.html.

Walter, John C., and J. Raymond Jones. 1989. *The Harlem Fox: J. Raymond Jones and Tammany, 1920–1970*. Albany: State University of New York Press.

Walters, Ronald W. 1988. *Black Presidential Politics in America: A Strategic Approach*. Albany: State University of New York Press.

Walton, Hanes. 1972. *Black Politics: A Theoretical and Structural Analysis*. Philadelphia: Lippincott.

Warner, Fred. 1901. *Michigan Official Director and Michigan Manual*. Lansing: Michigan State Legislature Legislative Service Bureau.

Weiss, Nancy Joan. 1983. *Farewell to the Party of Lincoln: Black Politics in the Age of FDR*. Princeton, NJ: Princeton University Press.

White, Katherine J. Curtis, Kyle Crowder, Stewart E. Tolnay, and Robert M. Adelman. 2005. "Race, Gender, and Marriage: Destination Selection during the Great Migration." *Demography* 42 (2): 215–241.

White, Theodore. 1956. "The Negro Voter: Can He Elect a President?" *Collier's*, August, 19. http://historymatters.gmu.edu/d/6331/. Accessed March 31, 2014.

Wilkerson, Isabel. 2010. *The Warmth of Other Suns: The Epic Story of America's Great Migration*. New York: Vintage.

Wilson, James Q. 1960. *Negro Politics: The Search for Leadership*. New York: Free Press.

Wolfinger, James. 2007. *Philadelphia Divided: Race and Politics in the City of Brotherly Love*. Chapel Hill: University of North Carolina Press.

Wood, Peter H. 2000. "Strange New Land: 1619–1776." In *To Make Our World Anew: A History of African Americans*, ed. Robin D. G. Kelley and Earl Lewis, 53–102. New York: Oxford University Press.

Woodson, Carter G. 1970. *A Century of Negro Migration*. New York: Dover.

Additional Sources

Boykin, Ulysses W. *A Hand Book on the Detroit Negro*. Detroit: Minority Study Associates, 1943.

Campbell, Angus, Philip Converse, Warren Miller, and Donald Stokes. *Elections and the Political Order*. New York: Wiley, 1966.

Capeci, Dominic J., Jr., ed. *Detroit and the "Good War": The World War II Letters of Mayor Edward Jeffries and Friends*. Lexington: University Press of Kentucky, 2015.

Dancy, John Campbell. *Sand against the Wind: The Memoirs of John C. Dancy*. Detroit: Wayne State University Press, 1966.

Foner, Eric. *Forever Free: The Story of Emancipation and Reconstruction*. New York: Knopf, 2006.

Green, Paul Michael, and Melvin G. Holli, eds. *The Mayors: The Chicago Political Tradition*. Carbondale: Southern Illinois University Press, 1987.

Grossman, Ron. "Ralph Metcalfe: Olympian with Jesse Owens Went on to Chicago Politics." *Chicago Tribune*, March 24, 2016. http://www.chicagotribune.com/news/history/ct-metcalfe-jesse-owens-race-olympics-flashback-perspec-0327-jm-20160324-story.html#. Accessed September 11, 2018.

Heckscher, August, and Phyllis C. Robinson. *When LaGuardia Was Mayor: New York's Legendary Years*. New York: Norton, 1978.

Lacey, Robert. *Ford: The Men and the Machine*. Boston: Little, Brown, 1986.

Landers, Jane. "Slavery in the Lower South." *OAH Magazine of History* 17, no. 3 (2003): 23–27.

Lapp, Rudolph M. *Blacks in Gold Rush California*. New Haven, CT: Yale University Press, 1977.

"A Legal Light." *The Colored American* (Washington, D.C.), October 8, 1904. *Chronicling America: Historic American Newspapers.* Library of Congress. http://chroniclingamerica.loc.gov/lccn/sn83027091/1904-10-08/ed-1/seq-2/.

Martelle, Scott. *Detroit: A Biography.* Chicago: Chicago Review Press, 2012.

Miller, Karen R. *Managing Inequality: Northern Racial Liberalism in Interwar Detroit.* New York: New York University Press, 2016.

Robinson, Tony, and Stephen Noriega. "Voter Migration as a Source of Electoral Change in the Rocky Mountain West." *Political Geography* 29, no. 1 (2010): 28–39.

Schickler, Eric, Kathryn Pearson, and Brian Feinstein. "Shifting Partisan Coalitions: Support for Civil Rights in Congress from 1933–1972." *Journal of Politics* 72, no. 3 (2010): 672–689.

Solomon, Thomas Ralph. "Participation of Negroes in Detroit Elections." Ph.D. diss., University of Michigan, 1939.

Turner, Arthur, and Earl R. Moses. *Colored Detroit: A Brief History of Detroit's Colored Population and a Directory of Their Businesses, Organizations, Professions and Trades.* Detroit: Burton Historical Collection, 1924.

Work, Monroe N. *Negro Year Book: An Annual Encyclopedia of the Negro 1918–1919.* Tuskegee, AL: Negro Year Book Publishing, 1918–1919.

Index

Page numbers in italics refer to figures.

Keneshia N. Grant is an Assistant Professor of Political Science at Howard University.